Yes You Are!

Thoughts and Scriptures to Speak Over Yourself and Others

Michael S. Smith

Foreword by Matthew Byrne

TRILOGY
PROFESSIONAL PUBLISHING MEETS POWERFUL PROMOTION
A wholly owned subsidiary of TBN

Yes You Are! Thoughts and Scriptures to Speak Over Yourself and Others

Trilogy Christian Publishers A Wholly Owned Subsidary of Trinity Broadcasting Network

2442 Michelle Drive Tustin, CA 92780

Cover design by: Grant Swank

For information about special discounts for bulk purchases, please contact Trilogy Christian Publishing.

Manufactured in the United States of America

10 9 8 7 6 5 4 3 2 1

Library of Congress Cataloging-in-Publication Data is available.

ISBN: 978-1-68556-793-4

E-ISBN: 978-1-68556-794-1

Dedication

First, I want to thank my Lord and Savior Jesus Christ for giving me the words to put in this book. Without You, none of this would have been possible. I give You all honor, glory, and praise. Thank You for loving me and for always being with me even in the toughest of times.

I also want to personally thank you for purchasing *Yes You Are! Thoughts and Scriptures to Speak Over Yourself and Others.* With all of the negativity in the world today, many people seem to have lost their hope and joy. My desire is to change that. That is why I decided to write this book. I pray that this book blesses, uplifts, and encourages you. I welcome your feedback. You may email me at yesyouare2021@gmail.com.

Thank you so much, and may God bless you richly!

—Michael S. Smith

Acknowledgments

I would like to thank some people who, throughout the time I have known them, have supported, encouraged, and inspired me. Without you, I wouldn't be where I am today. There are many others who may not be listed here, but I want to thank you as well. I will forever be grateful to each one of you.

Helen Brock. Mom, you were the greatest mom any child could ask for. You always loved me and never criticized me or ran me down. When I was being bullied as a child, you always had the right words to say. I remember you telling me to ignore them, and, eventually, they'll leave you alone. You would always lovingly encourage me. I wish I would have gotten to spend more time with you the last several years of your life, but distance made it difficult to do. I will never forget the lessons you taught me and will be forever grateful for you. Thank you, Mom. I love you.

Leon and Renee Patillo. I have been listening to Leon's music since the 1980s, and I could always feel the spirit of the Lord in every song he sang. For those who may have never heard of him, he used to be the lead singer for the band Santana. Then the Lord touched him, and he has been writing inspiring Christian music ever since. In February 2020, he and his wife Renee reached out to me to show me how I could live a better life and to have a business when I can help others do the same. The love and support that both of you have given me have been nothing short of amazing. Thank you for all that you do and for not giving up on me like so many others have.

Pastors Joe and Rachel Moon. I met Joe and Rachel in September of 2020 when I moved to Wyoming. They pastor a church called River of Life Fellowship. When I was moving into my house, I thought I was going to have to unload the U-Haul by myself. I was told about Joe by the person who runs the hotel that we were staying in. I contacted him and asked if he knew anyone that could help me. He was one of the first people who arrived to help me plus enlisted the help of others, so it made the process a lot easier. I began attending their church, where Joe preaches about service to others and the power of prayer in our lives. Your words have uplifted and encouraged me, and I wanted to thank you.

Matthew Byrne. You are a true inspiration to me. You are a great friend and brother in Christ, and I'm blessed to know you. I greatly appreciate you writing the amazing foreword to this book. When I had hit a wall in the writing of this book, you encouraged me to finish it, and I will be forever grateful for that. Thank you for all you do and for being such a blessing in my life.

Pastors Loren and Beth Sanford. I first met Loren and Beth when I began to attend their church back in 2007. They pastor a church called New Song Fellowship in Denver. His music and his sermons are unlike much of what I had listened to in the past, and they still are. Loren went to be with the Lord in 2020. I learned that I need to follow the heart of Father God and not be caught up in how the world thinks. Your Daily Word that you were doing on Facebook has helped to remind me to continue to focus on God and His ways. I want to thank you both for being an inspiration in my life.

My children—April, Michael, Jamie, and Robbie. I thank God for each of you. I was not always the kind of dad that you deserved, yet throughout the many dark times in my life when I wanted to give up, you were one of the reasons that kept me going. Thank you!

To all my other family and friends (you know who you are) who have supported and encouraged me throughout my life, thank you!

I dedicate this book to each of you and to the many others who I pray will read this book and be forever changed in a good way.

Content

Foreword

When Michael told me he was needing someone to write his foreword to his book but didn't know who, I instantly felt like God was telling me that I should write it. But I figured that it was just my vanity speaking because, after all, "Who am I?" Well, who am I? I am a son of the Most High God, just like all who believe in Christ Jesus as their Lord and Savior! At twenty-four years old, I came to Christ in a very small southern Baptist church in Lee's Summit, Missouri. I had a couple of close buddies that invited me to a Bible study for young adults on a Thursday night. That night after reading the Word of God out loud, something inside of me connected with it, and I asked the pastor leading the study why I felt that way all of a sudden. He began to lead me to Christ. That night, I asked Jesus to come into my heart and be my Lord and Savior, and, boy, were things different from that point on. Well, that was in August of 1999, and I haven't stopped pursuing God and everything He has for me every day since. Now I will say that my relationship with the Holy King has gotten better since I've learned to build His kingdom instead of my own. But it wasn't always sunshine and roses following God; not saying that it's that way now, but I've matured a lot over the years, although I still consider myself a young man. As the youngest of five children, I watched my parents struggle and become alcoholics because of the stresses that life brings as well as unresolved issues from both of my parents' childhoods that shaped them for the worst. They always walked around with their secret pain that they never talked about.

Going through childhood along with my siblings, we all struggled not knowing who we were or where our strengths were. My parents split up and divorced when I was five years old—the toll of drinking and fighting finally came crashing down. Fortunately, both my parents sobered up after the divorce and were sober for the rest of their days. I had a good relationship with both my mother and father, who have both passed on. But with an unresolved childhood, I spent many years stumbling around and making foolish mistakes.

Whether it was money or women, I faltered and failed at both. The one thing our parents gave us was a good work ethic, so I always excelled with employers, but not so much with almost every other aspect of my life.

So, when I came to the Lord in 1999, I thought my life was going to get exponentially better; boy, was I in for a treat. In defense of the Lord, of course my life got much better, but what I didn't realize was I was about to get remade in every way possible. As I started to live for the Lord, I had this nagging identity crisis. God started to show me that I wasn't who I thought I was, and I'm becoming who my younger self didn't like. With all my heart, I didn't want to become one of those "do-gooder Christians" who, to me, seemed as fake as could be. But at the same time, I was struggling at becoming the man my father was. So here I sat in this giant valley of my life, on one side, my family identity, and on the other, my new identity in Christ. All the while, I kept asking God, "Who am I?" and "What was I made to do?" Well, here comes a one-sentence sermon: if you play in the mud, you're going to get dirty! As a new believer, I was living for

Jesus when it was convenient and living for myself when it suited my needs. Well, I had the old illustration of the devil on one shoulder and Jesus on the other. I was trying to live in two worlds, and you all know how that goes, not very well. I was being torn apart by my own selfish decisions; at that moment in my life, I wish I would have had somebody hand me a book that spoke to who I was by the word of God. I wish I had a resource that helped me speak out what my soul was crying about! I wanted to move forward with God. I wanted to make the right decisions for my life; I wanted to walk away from my past and leave it far behind. But the voices of my past were louder at that time in my life than the truth of God, or I was listening to them instead of listening to God. My past as a young adult and my past as a child of an alcoholic home said that I wasn't worth messing with or investing in. Every time I would try to take steps to improve my life, it always seemed like two steps forward and three steps back, never getting ahead and never leaving my past behind.

I looked at what God put in Michael's heart and was poured out on paper, and I think back to those days as a young man, confused and seemingly torn between two lives, never believing I was worthy of love or approval. I wish I would have had this book in those days, speaking over myself daily the truth of how God feels about me. Speaking over myself the truth of "who I am," my purpose of why I was born, and how incredibly in love God is with me. Since my younger days in the Lord, I have been ordained as a minister and have traveled to six different countries preaching and teaching the gospel of Jesus Christ. I've seen the lame walk, deaf ears open, and body parts grow back. I have seen food supernaturally multiplied to feed the many who came to hear and see God! I've seen thousands of men, women, and children come to the Lord. My favorite ministry out of all the things the Lord asked me to do is ministering to men, young and old, and telling them the truth about who they are. *Yes You Are! Thoughts and Scriptures to Speak Over Yourself and Others* is a great tool for those who have questions about "who they are." I love Michael's story and testimony of how he has overcome many difficulties and trials in his life and is still moving forward with the dream and message God has put in his heart. You can get a feel for how Michael and many others are overcoming their past and the lies spoken about them by declaring over themselves who they are in Christ, by the Word of God! To be encouraged by people is always a comfort, but to read the Word of God and believe what is being said about you is such a faith-building adventure that you will not be the same; you'll be forever changed in your heart and mind.

My parting encouragement to you is *Yes You Are!*

—Matthew Byrne

Introduction

I would like to start out with a little bit about myself. Throughout my life, I have suffered from emotional abuse, either being bullied as a child or in relationships that I have been in. That resulted in spending a lot of time alone because I didn't want to get hurt. I found that as time went on, I began to wonder if what people were saying to me was true. I wouldn't really say anything good about myself because of it. In the past couple of years, God began speaking to me and told me that I was made in His image and reminded me of Psalm 139, verses 13 and 14, which says, "I knew you before I formed you in your mother's womb. I praise you because I am fearfully and wonderfully made." God told me that He was pleased with His creation and still is today, and He loves me just as much now as when He created me. I believe that many people who will read this book have gone through similar experiences at some point in their life. I have good news for you. What God reminded me of in that verse is true of you as well. Jesus said that the world hated Him before they hated us. It doesn't matter how the world feels about us. What matters is that we know that God has loved us from the very beginning and will continue loving us throughout eternity. This we can always count on even when we can't always count on others.

Proverbs 18 verse 21 says, "The power of life and death are in the tongue and those that love it will eat its fruit." Many times, others have spoken words of death to us, and we have even done that to ourselves. We make a mistake and start beating ourselves up and call ourselves stupid or worthless or something else which couldn't be further from the truth. It's time to change that mentality. A piece of advice that I give to people is, "Whenever you make a mistake, use it as a learning tool, not a beat-me-up session." Satan wants us to beat ourselves up so he can steal our joy. Instead of saying bad things about yourself, start saying, "Well, that didn't work. What can I do differently next time?" Start speaking words of life over yourself, such as "I am somebody," "I do matter," or "I am loved." When you change what you say about yourself to life-giving words, it will start to flow out to the people around you, and you will start speaking words of life to them too. The Bible says that all have sinned and fallen short of the glory of God, which means no one is perfect, but God still loves us anyway. Before you say anything negative or hurtful to someone, ask yourself if you would like that same thing said to you. I'm sure you will say no. I encourage you to get in the habit of speaking life-giving words to yourself and everyone you know. It could just be the one thing that can turn someone's day completely around or even your own.

My prayer is that every scripture, declaration, and prayer in this book will encourage you and uplift you. Read each one out loud. I've heard that when you hear what you are reading has more of an impact than just reading the words alone. Thank you for reading this book, and may God bless you richly.

Chapter 1

Speak Life

Twenty-One-Gun Salute

Our words are powerful! I'll say it again: *our words are powerful!* The words we speak start out as a thought that enters our mind and eventually come out of our mouths. Thoughts come from one of two places, either God or Satan. God's words are positive, and Satan's words are negative. Our words can either build us up (positive words) or tear us down (negative words). The words that we speak to others can have the same effect.

Proverbs 18:21 tells us just how powerful our words are: "The power of life and death are in the tongue and those that love it will eat its fruit."

Most people have probably heard of something called a twenty-one-gun salute. That is where seven military members fire three shots each into the air to celebrate something good or to pay tribute so someone who made an impact. This same analogy can be applied in a biblical sense to our words. Instead of the traditional meaning of a twenty-one salute, I want you to think of it in a different way. What are your words worthy of? Are they worth twenty-one angels singing praise to God for them, or are they worth twenty-one demons shooting fiery darts at you? Do your words deserve twenty-one people shooting guns in the air in praise of what you said, or twenty-one guns pointed at you for the hateful and hurtful things you said? Ouch! That puts a completely different perspective on what we think or say, doesn't it? I will be the first to admit here that my words often have not been ones deserving of twenty-one angels singing praises to God for them or twenty-one people shooting guns in the air. I'm a hundred percent certain that pretty much everyone who reads this book will either say the same thing or they will completely deny it, just like Peter did when Jesus said, "Before the rooster crows, you will deny me three times," which is exactly what he did. And when the rooster crowed, he realized that Jesus had spoken the truth about him, and he went outside of the courtyard and wept bitterly. Does that describe any of us? I know it does me more often than I want to admit.

So how do we change that? The Bible talks about a thought that comes into our minds, which will come out of our mouths. Positive thoughts come from God, and negative thoughts come from Satan. You have two options. You can accept the thought that comes into your mind, or you can reject it. Change what you allow into your mind that will come out of your mouth, and you will not only change your own life but also the lives of your family, your friends, your coworkers, your neighbors, your city, your state, your country, and even the world.

The following is true about the words we speak:

They can create, or they can destroy.

They can be beneficial, or they can be detrimental.

They are loving, or they are hateful.

They can build up, or they can tear down.

They can bring joy, or they can bring sorrow.

They can hurt, or they can heal.

They can bring comfort, or they can cause pain.

They can create success, or they can create failure.

We have the choice to either speak words of life or words of death to ourselves and others. I challenge you to always speak words of life.

When you realize how powerful your words are and the potential they have to positively or negatively affect people, places, and things, you have the ability to change what you allow in your mind that will come out of your mouth. Until you realize the power of your words and the impact they can have not only on others around you but even on yourself, your words will never change.

I have this saying: *Whatever follows your "I am" statements determines who you are or who you will become. Why not say positive words to yourself every day!*

Put Down Those Stones

Did you know that stones come in many different forms? For most of history, including in Jesus' day, the only stones there that existed were verbal or physical stones. Today, there are not only those stones but also social media and other stones as well. Jesus said in Matthew 12:34, "For out of the abundance of the heart the mouth speaks." Satan knows this and uses a variety of ways to put negative, ungodly thoughts into our minds which includes family, friends, coworkers, other people including Christians, TV, radio, the Internet, and more. Those ungodly thoughts are stones, which will at some point come out of our mouths and be hurled at others. We will even hurl those stones at ourselves. Instead of focusing on the things of God like we should be doing, we instead find ourselves focusing on things that do not bless us or others in any way. We need to change that. We need to focus on the only truth, which is the Word of God.

A perfect example of verbal stones being thrown is found in John 8, verses 2 to 11, which says,

> At dawn he appeared again in the temple courts, where all the people gathered around him, and he sat down to teach them. The teachers of the law and the Pharisees brought in a woman caught in adultery. They made her stand before the group and said to Jesus, "Teacher, this woman was caught in the act of adultery. In the Law Moses commanded us to stone such women. Now what do you say?" They were using this question as a trap to have a basis for accusing him. But Jesus bent down and started to write on the ground with his finger. When they kept on questioning him, he straightened up and said to them, "Let any one of you who is without sin be the first to throw a stone at her." Again, he stooped down and wrote on the ground. At this, those who heard began to go away one at a time, the older ones first, until only Jesus was left, with the woman still standing there. Jesus straightened up and asked her, "Woman, where are they? Has no one condemned you?" "No one, sir," she said. "Then neither do I condemn you," Jesus declared. "Go now and leave your life of sin."

The Pharisees used the verbal stones of judgment to justify using physical stones at this woman. How many times has any of us used verbal stones in our lifetime? I can't even begin to count the number of times that I've done it.

Positive Thoughts

Your thoughts have a lot of power. They can put a smile on your face, or they can bring you down. Just like words, thoughts can be life-giving to the person thinking them, or they can take you to the point where you think your life has no meaning and you want to end it. Negative thoughts are from our spiritual enemy. He wants us to think that we're worthless or not good enough. Positive thoughts are from God. There are positive thoughts all throughout the Bible. I encourage you whenever you feel any negative thoughts creeping into your mind to take authority over them and kick them out and then open your Bible and start reading all the good things that God has to say about you.

Philippians 4:8 tells us what we should always think about: "Finally, brothers and sisters, whatever is true, whatever is noble, whatever is right, whatever is pure, whatever is lovely, whatever is admirable, if anything is excellent or praiseworthy, think about such things."

Protect Yourself

Satan is always trying to put negative thoughts into our minds. He has a variety of ways to do that. He will use people or circumstances to try to slip those thoughts into our mind. We must be on guard constantly against his schemes. If we don't, he will get those types of thoughts in there. Whenever he tries to use a person to do it, tell that person, "I don't receive that. I choose to believe what God's Word says about me." Then walk away. Satan would love nothing more than to get two people into an argument. Don't let him lure you into that trap. If something bad is happening to you, rather than allowing negative thoughts to control you, pray and turn that situation over to God. Ask Him for wisdom on how to handle that situation and what His Word says.

Paul tells us in Ephesians 6:10–20 how we can protect ourselves from the negative thoughts that Satan tries to put in our minds:

> Finally, be strong in the Lord and in his mighty power. Put on the full armor of God, so that you can take your stand against the devil's schemes. For our struggle is not against flesh and blood, but against the rulers, against the authorities, against the powers of this dark world, and against the spiritual forces of evil in the heavenly realms. Therefore, put on the full armor of God, so that when the day of evil comes, you may be able to stand your ground, and after you have done everything, to stand. Stand firm then, with the belt of truth buckled around your waist, with the breastplate of righteousness in place, and with your feet fitted with the readiness that comes from the gospel of peace. In addition to all this, take up the shield of faith, with which you can extinguish all the flaming arrows of the evil one. Take the helmet of salvation and the sword of the Spirit, which is the word of God. And pray in the Spirit on all occasions with all kinds of prayers and requests. Be alert and always keep on praying for all the Lord's people. Pray also for me, that whenever I speak, words may be given me so that I will fearlessly

make known the mystery of the gospel, for which I am an ambassador in chains. Pray that I may declare it fearlessly, as I should.

Kick the Devil Out of Your Head

We have established that negative thoughts are not from God. Another way that we can stop negative thoughts from entering our minds is to resist them. Use the authority of Jesus' name to send the devil running with his thoughts in the opposite direction. Always be on guard because he'll be back to try something else. When he does, keep using the authority that was given to you as many times as you need to.

James 4:7 also tells us how we can prevent negative thoughts from entering our minds: "Resist the devil and he must flee."

It's important to always remember that the thoughts we allow into our minds eventually become words.

Lessons Learned

Have you ever made a mistake or two in your life only to beat yourself up over it or have other people beat you up for it? I know that I personally have made too many mistakes in my life to count them all. You may have as well. I want you to know this one thing: *We are not the sum total of our mistakes.* We are who God's Word says we are. Mistakes are a part of life, and we all make them. Romans 3:23 says, "For all have sinned and fallen short of the glory of God." The awesome thing is that when we make a mistake, we have an awesome and loving God who is more than willing to forgive us when we ask Him. First Kings 8:50 says, "And forgive your people, who have sinned against you, forgive all the offenses they have committed against you, and cause their captors to show them mercy." You are allowed to forgive yourself as well. Never hang on to past mistakes nor let anyone make you feel like you're less of a person because of those mistakes. You are who God says you are and nothing less. I have a saying that I created many years ago: *Never use your mistakes as a beat-me-up session; use them as a learning tool to do things differently next time.*

Instead of calling yourself an idiot or worse, say to yourself, "Well, that didn't work. What can I do differently next time." Use your mistakes as an opportunity for growth in the Lord, not as a shaming session, which is exactly what Satan wants you to do.

God Created You

Did you know that God has known you forever? Psalm 139:13–14 says, "For you created my inmost being, you knit me together in my mother's womb. I praise you because I am fearfully and wonderfully made."

I know that many people are struggling emotionally, physically, and spiritually for a variety of reasons, but I want to encourage you today! I want you to always remember these five things:

You are somebody!

You do matter!

You are loved!

You are a person of extreme value and significance!
You are fearfully and wonderfully made!

You Are Somebody!

Psalm 139, verses 13–14, says, "God created our inmost being and he knit us together in our mother's womb. I praise you because I am fearfully and wonderfully made, your works are wonderful, I know that full well."

That means that He knew us before He ever spoke the world into existence. Because He did that, that automatically makes us somebody because He took the time to create us. When He had finished creating us, He took a step back and saw just how good His creation was, and He was well pleased with it. Can I tell you something? He still is pleased to this very day and will be until we see Him again.

You Do Matter!

The world may think that we're a nobody, but that's simply not true. We are somebody because He made us. Many of us at some point in our lives have been told that we don't matter or we will never amount to anything. When I was a child, I was bullied many times by children who simply did not know or weren't taught any better. Because of that, I spent a lot of time alone just so I wouldn't have to hear those words. Even in my adult life, I was criticized, judged, manipulated, controlled, and guilt-tripped in the relationships I was in. I began to believe that everything people were saying to me was who I am as a person. I had no idea that none of what was being said to me was true.

During our adult lives, we may hear negative things like that from people we know, whether it is family, a stranger, coworkers, even our boss or our spouse. After a while, we begin to believe those things, and so we get discouraged and stop trying, or we start saying things like that to others. Not one of the cruel and hurtful things that people say to us or about us is true, and we should never allow ourselves to say those things to others. The fact that God took the time to create us speaks the exact opposite. Even when you hear negative words, I encourage you to remind yourself of what God's Word says in Psalm 139 and to tell yourself that according to God's Word, I am somebody, and I do matter, and nothing anyone could ever say to me will overrule that and that I won't speak those kinds of words to others.

You Are Loved!

John 3:16 says, "For God so loved the world that he sent his only begotten son that whoever believes in him shall not perish but have eternal life." Just that verse alone should be enough to put a smile on our face knowing that God loves us that much to send Jesus into this world and then allow Him to be nailed to a cross to die for our sins. Pastor Robert Gelinas put it this way, "God loves you, and there's nothing about it." Even when we feel alone or unloved in this world, God still loves us. He has loved us from the moment He formed us and put us in our mother's womb. He still loves us today and will love us throughout eternity. There is nothing that you can do that will make Him love you any less than He does right now. The Bible says that all have sinned and fallen short of the glory of God. Just because we committed a sin doesn't mean that God is going to stop loving us. He's waiting on us to confess our sins to Him and seek His forgiveness, and He will forgive us every time. Once we have confessed the sin and sought His forgiveness, we should never repeat the sin again. I like to put it this way, "Instead of using your mistake or sin as a beat-me-up session, use it as a learning tool instead." Ask yourself, "What can I do differently next time?" It's far too easy for us to call ourselves stupid or worthless. We need to change that mentality and instead start reminding ourselves that God loves us, we are somebody to Him, and we are valued by Him.

You Are a Person of Extreme Value and Significance!

Throughout my life, I have suffered from emotional abuse, either being bullied as a child or in relationships that I have been in. That resulted in spending a lot of time alone because I didn't want to get hurt. I found that as time went on, I began to wonder if what people were saying to me was true. I wouldn't really see myself as valuable or significant because of it. In the past couple of years, God began speaking to me and told me that I was made in His image and reminded me of Psalm 139, verses 13 and 14. God told me that He was pleased with His creation and still is today, and He loves me just as much now as when He created me. I believe that many of you have gone through similar experiences at some point in your life. I have good news for you. What God reminded me of in that verse is true of you as well. He sees you as valuable and significant since He was the one who created you.

You Are Fearfully and Wonderfully Made!

God tells us in verse 14 that we are fearfully and wonderfully made. That alone is enough of a reason for us to praise Him. He made us, and He is pleased with what He made. The world may not think that we are fearfully and wonderfully made, but God does. Even when we don't feel that way because of things that are going on or that we have done in our life, it does not make that any less true. You really are fearfully and wonderfully made. God already said it, and that will never change. Never forget that!

Declarations

Read these declarations out loud. I will have more declarations in a later chapter of this book.

I declare in *Jesus'* name that I am a masterpiece, I am loved, and I am a person of extreme value and significance!

I declare in *Jesus'* name that when God created me, He was well pleased with His creation and still is today!

I declare in *Jesus'* name that I am fearfully and wonderfully made. I am a child of God!

Change Your Words, Change Your Life

What kind of words do you speak to yourself and others every day?

The Bible says out of the heart, the mouth speaks. When we change the thoughts that we allow in our minds to life-giving ones, then our whole attitude toward ourselves and others will change.

I encourage you to begin speaking positive thoughts and scriptures out loud every day.

When you change your words to life-giving ones, you will change your life.

The next chapter is called "Thank You, God." Each page starts off with "I thank You, God, that..." followed by "I Am" or "You Are" life-giving thoughts and then a Scripture verse that you can speak over yourself or others. There is also space where you can take notes on how each one spoke to or impacted you. I encourage you to take advantage of that part.

Chapter 2

Thank You, God

Give Thanks

What are you thankful for in your life? In your prayer time, do you regularly thank God for the good things that He says about you or has done for you? It's important that we give God all the credit for those things. When we just think things like "I'm so lucky" or "Because of what I've done, I have this big house or nice car" or some other thing, we give ourselves credit for something instead of giving God all the credit. We open the door for pride to creep in. The Bible talks a lot about pride and how it comes before a fall, so I encourage you to give credit where credit is due, and that is to God, who created each one of us. When we make a point of thanking God for what we have or what we have become, it's not a sign of weakness; it's a sign of humility. God loves it when we acknowledge Him for who we are or what we have. Even if you don't believe you have anything to be thankful for, rather than focusing on the negative things happening in your life, thank God anyway in advance of the good things that He is going to bring into your life and believe by faith that those things will come.

Each page contains a prayer of thanksgiving. There is also a space for notes where you can write down what God was saying to you through that prayer. I encourage you to read them out loud. Hearing yourself read each one can have more of an impact than just reading them alone. You can even raise your hands as a sign of submission to God when you read them. Read several at a time. Do this daily and watch how God will transform your life by the renewing of your mind.

I thank You, God, that...

I am victorious in every battle!

For Your Word says in Exodus 14:14,

"The Lord will fight for you; you need only to be still."

Notes:

_____

_____

_____

_____

_____

_____

_____

_____

_____

I thank You, God, that...

You bless me!

For Your Word says in Numbers 6:24–26,

"The Lord bless you and keep you, the Lord make his face to shine on you and be gracious to you, the Lord turns his face toward you and give you his peace."

Notes:

_____

_____

_____

_____

_____

_____

_____

_____

_____

I thank You, God, that...
I love You with all my being!
For Your Word says in Deuteronomy 6:5,
"Love the Lord your God with all your heart and with all your soul and with all your strength."

Notes:

_____

_____

_____

_____

_____

_____

_____

_____

_____

I thank You, God, that...

I am empowered to prosper!

For Your Word says in Deuteronomy 8:18,

"But remember the Lord your God, for it is he who gives you the ability to produce wealth, and so confirms his covenant, which he swore to your ancestors, as it is today."

Notes:

_____

_____

_____

_____

_____

_____

_____

_____

_____

I thank You, God, that...

I am generous!

For Your Word says in Deuteronomy 15:10,

"Give generously to them and do so without a grudging heart; then because of this the Lord your God will bless you in all your work and in everything you put your hand to."

Notes:

_____

_____

_____

_____

_____

_____

_____

_____

_____

I thank You, God, that...

I am the head and not the tail!

For Your Word says in Deuteronomy 28:13,

"The Lord will make you the head, not the tail. If you pay attention to the commands of the Lord your God that I give you this day and carefully follow them, you will always be at the top, never at the bottom."

Notes:

_____

_____

_____

_____

_____

_____

_____

_____

I thank You, God, that...

You are always with me!

For Your Word says in Deuteronomy 31:6,

"Be strong and courageous. Do not be afraid or terrified because of them, for the Lord your God goes with you; he will never leave you nor forsake you."

Notes:

_____

_____

_____

_____

_____

_____

_____

_____

_____

I thank You, God, that...

You are faithful!

For Your Word says in Deuteronomy 32:3–4,

"I will proclaim the name of the Lord. Oh, praise the greatness of our God! He is the Rock, his works are perfect, and all his ways are just. A faithful God who does no wrong, upright, and just is he."

Notes:

_____

_____

_____

_____

_____

_____

_____

_____

_____

I thank You, God, that...

I am courageous!

For Your Word says in Joshua 1:9,

"Have I not commanded you? Be strong and courageous. Do not be afraid; do not be discouraged, for the Lord your God will be with you wherever you go."

Notes:

_____

_____

_____

_____

_____

_____

_____

_____

_____

I thank You, God, that...

I am a giant slayer like David!

For Your Word says in 1 Samuel 17:45,

"David said to the Philistine, 'You come against me with a sword and spear and javelin, but I come against you in the name of the Lord Almighty, the God of the armies of Israel, whom you have defied.'"

Notes:

_____

_____

_____

_____

_____

_____

_____

_____

I thank You, God, that...

You have heard my prayers!

For Your Word says in 2 Kings 20:5,

"Go back and tell Hezekiah, the ruler of my people, this is what the Lord, the God of your father David says: I have heard your prayers, and seen your tears, I will heal you."

Notes:

_____

_____

_____

_____

_____

_____

_____

_____

_____

I thank You, God, that...

I am humble!

For Your Word says in 2 Chronicles 7:14,

"If my people, who are called by my name, will humble themselves and pray and seek my face and turn from their wicked ways, then I will hear from heaven, and I will forgive their sin and heal their land."

Notes:

_____

_____

_____

_____

_____

_____

_____

_____

I thank You, God, that...

I have Your joy!

For Your Word says in Nehemiah 8:10,

"Do not grieve, for the joy of the Lord is your strength."

Notes:

_____

_____

_____

_____

_____

_____

_____

_____

_____

I thank You, God, that...

Everything I touch prospers!

For Your Word says in Psalm 1:3,

"That person is like a tree planted by streams of water, which yields its fruit in season and who's leaf does not wither, whatever they do prospers."

Notes:

_____

_____

_____

_____

_____

_____

_____

_____

_____

I thank You, God, that...

I am surrounded with Your favor!

For Your Word says in Psalm 5:12,

"Sure, Lord, you bless the righteous; you surround them with your favor as with a shield."

Notes:

_____

_____

_____

_____

_____

_____

_____

_____

_____

_____

I thank You, God, that...
I rejoice in Your salvation!
For Your Word says in Psalm 13:5–6,
"But I trust in your unfailing love, my heart rejoices in your salvation.
I will sing the Lord's praise, for he has been good to me."

Notes:

_____

_____

_____

_____

_____

_____

_____

_____

I thank You, God, that...
I am the apple of Your eye!
For Your Word says in Psalm 17:8,
"Keep me as the apple of your eye, hide me in the shadow of your wings."

Notes:

_____

_____

_____

_____

_____

_____

_____

_____

_____

I thank You, God, that...

You are my rock!

For Your Word says in Psalm 18:2,

"The Lord is my rock, my fortress, and my deliverer; my God is my rock, in whom I take refuge, my shield and the horn of my salvation, my stronghold."

Notes:

_____

_____

_____

_____

_____

_____

_____

_____

_____

I thank You, God, that...

I am saved from my enemies!

For Your Word says in Psalm 18:3,

"I called to the Lord who is worth of praise, and I have been saved from my enemies."

Notes:

_____

_____

_____

_____

_____

_____

_____

_____

_____

I thank You, God, that...
You rescued me!
For Your Word says in Psalm 18:17,
"He rescued me from my powerful enemy, from my foes, who were too strong for me."

Notes:

_____

_____

_____

_____

_____

_____

_____

_____

_____

I thank You, God, that...

I am secure!

For Your Word says in Psalm 18:32,

"It is God who arms me with strength and keeps my way secure."

Notes:

_____

_____

_____

_____

_____

_____

_____

_____

_____

I thank You, God, that...

I am anointed!

For Your Word says in Psalm 20:6,

"Now this I know: The Lord gives victory to his anointed. He answers from his heavenly sanctuary with the victorious power of his right hand."

Notes:

_____

_____

_____

_____

_____

_____

_____

_____

I thank You, God, that...
You are my shepherd!
For Your Word says in Psalm 23:1,
"The Lord is my shepherd, I lack nothing."

Notes:

_____

_____

_____

_____

_____

_____

_____

_____

I thank You, God, that...

You lead me!

For Your Word says in Psalm 23:2,

"He makes me lie down in green pastures, he leads me besides quiet waters."

Notes:

_____

_____

_____

_____

_____

_____

_____

_____

I thank You, God, that...

You refresh me and guide me!

For Your Word says in Psalm 23:3,

"He refreshes my soul. He guides me along the right paths for his name's sake."

Notes:

_____

_____

_____

_____

_____

_____

_____

_____

I thank You, God, that...
I do not fear evil!
For Your Word says in Psalm 23:4,
"Even though I walk through the darkest valley, I will fear no evil, for you are with me; your rod and your staff, they comfort me."

Notes:

_____

_____

_____

_____

_____

_____

_____

_____

I thank You, God, that...

You have prepared my table!

For Your Word says in Psalm 23:5,

"You prepare a table before me in the presence of my enemies. You anoint my head with oil, my cup overflows."

Notes:

_____

_____

_____

_____

_____

_____

_____

_____

_____

I thank You, God, that...
Your goodness and love follow me!
For Your Word says in Psalm 23:6,
"Surely your goodness and love will follow me all the days of my life and I will dwell in the house of the Lord forever."

Notes:

_____

_____

_____

_____

_____

_____

_____

_____

I thank You, God, that...

You are my light and my salvation!

For Your Word says in Psalm 27:1,

"The Lord is my light and my salvation, whom shall I fear. The Lord is the stronghold of my life, of whom shall I be afraid."

Notes:

_____

_____

_____

_____

_____

_____

_____

_____

I thank You, God, that...

I am confident!

For Your Word says in Psalm 27:3,

"Though an army besiege me, my heart will not fear; though war breakout against me, even then I will be confident."

Notes:

_____

_____

_____

_____

_____

_____

_____

_____

I thank You, God, that...
You give me strength and peace!
For Your Word says in Psalm 29:11,
"The Lord gives strength to his people, the Lord blesses his people with peace."

Notes:

_____

_____

_____

_____

_____

_____

_____

_____

I thank You, God, that...

I have Your favor!

For Your Word says in Psalm 30:5,

"For His anger lasts only a moment, but his favor lasts a lifetime; weeping may stay for the night, but rejoicing comes in the morning."

Notes:

_____

_____

_____

_____

_____

_____

_____

_____

I thank You, God, that...

I dance with joy!

For Your Word says in Psalm 30:11–12,

"You have turned my wailing into dancing; you have removed my sackcloth and clothed me with joy, that my heart may sing your praises and not be silent. Lord my God, I will praise you forever."

Notes:

_____

_____

_____

_____

_____

_____

_____

_____

_____

_____

I thank You, God, that...

You give abundantly!

For Your Word says in Psalm 31:19,

"How abundant are the good things that you have stored up for those who fear you, that you bestow in the site of all, on those who take refuge in you."

Notes:

_____

_____

_____

_____

_____

_____

_____

_____

I thank You, God, that...

Your eyes are on me!

For Your Word says in Psalm 33:18,

"But the eyes of the Lord are on those who fear him, on those whose hope is in his unfailing love."

Notes:

_____

_____

_____

_____

_____

_____

_____

_____

I thank You, God, that...

I can always praise You!

For Your Word says in Psalm 34:1,

"I will always praise the Lord; his praise will always be on my lips!"

Notes:

_____

_____

_____

_____

_____

_____

_____

_____

I thank You, God, that...
I can glorify You!
For Your Word says in Psalm 34:3,
"Glorify the Lord with me, let us exalt his name together."

Notes:

_____

_____

_____

_____

_____

_____

_____

_____

I thank You, God, that...

You delivered me from my fears!

For Your Word says in Psalm 34:4,

"I sought the Lord, and he answered me, he delivered me from all my fears."

Notes:

_____

_____

_____

_____

_____

_____

_____

_____

_____

I thank You, God, that...

You are good!

For Your Word says in Psalm 34:8,

"Taste and see that the Lord is good, blessed is the one who takes refuge in him."

Notes:

_____

_____

_____

_____

_____

_____

_____

_____

I thank You, God, that...

You hear my cry!

For Your Word says in Psalm 34:15,

"The eyes of the Lord are on the righteous, and his ears are attentive to their cry."

Notes:

_____

_____

_____

_____

_____

_____

_____

_____

I thank You, God, that...
You give me the desires of my heart!
For Your Word says in Psalm 37:4,
"Take delight in the Lord, and he will give you the desires of your heart."

Notes:

_____

_____

_____

_____

_____

_____

_____

_____

_____

I thank You, God, that...
You make my steps firm!
For Your Word says in Psalm 37:23,
"The Lord makes firm the steps of the one who delights in Him."

Notes:

_____

_____

_____

_____

_____

_____

_____

_____

I thank You, God, that...

I exalt You!

For Your Word says in Psalm 46:10,

"He says, 'Be still and know that I am God, I will be exalted among the nations, I will be exalted in the earth.'"

Notes:

_____

_____

_____

_____

_____

_____

_____

_____

I thank You, God, that...

You are my refuge and my strong tower!

For Your Word says in Psalm 61:1–3,

"Hear my cry, O God, listen to my prayer. From the ends of the earth I call to you. I call as my heart grows faint, lead me to the rock that is higher than I. For you have been my refuge and a strong tower against the foe."

Notes:

_____

_____

_____

_____

_____

_____

_____

_____

I thank You, God, that...

I can sing praises unto You!

For Your Word says in Psalm 69:30,

"I will praise the name of God with song and shall magnify him with thanksgiving."

Notes:

_____

_____

_____

_____

_____

_____

_____

_____

_____

I thank You, God, that...
I am healthy and strong!
For Your Word says in Psalm 73:4,
"They have no struggles; their bodies are healthy and strong."

Notes:

_____

_____

_____

_____

_____

_____

_____

_____

I thank You, God, that...

You always give me good things!

For Your Word says in Psalm 84:11,

"For the Lord God is a sun and shield; the Lord bestows favor and honor, no good thing does he withhold from those whose walk is blameless."

Notes:

_____

_____

_____

_____

_____

_____

_____

_____

_____

I thank You, God, that...

You are my refuge and my fortress!

For Your Word says in Psalm 91:1–2,

"Whoever dwells in the shelter of the Most High, will rest in the shadow of the Almighty. I will say of the Lord, 'He is my refuge and my fortress, my God, in whom I trust.'"

Notes:

_____

_____

_____

_____

_____

_____

_____

_____

_____

I thank You, God, that...
Your angels guard me!
For Your Word says in Psalm 91:11,
"For he will command his angels concerning you to guard you in all your ways."

Notes:

_____

_____

_____

_____

_____

_____

_____

_____

_____

_____

I thank You, God, that...

You deliver me and honor me!

For Your Word says in Psalm 91:15,

"He will call on me, and I will answer him; I will be with him in trouble, I will deliver him and honor him."

Notes:

_____

_____

_____

_____

_____

_____

_____

_____

I thank You, God, that...

Your love endures forever!

For Your Word says in Psalm 100:5,

"For the Lord is good and His love endures forever. His faithfulness continues through all generations."

Notes:

_____

_____

_____

_____

_____

_____

_____

_____

_____

_____

I thank You, God, that...

For all Your benefits!

For Your Word says in Psalm 103:2–5,

"Praise the Lord, my soul, and forget not all his benefits, who forgives all your sins and heals all your diseases, who redeems your life from the pit and crowns you with love and compassion, who satisfies your desires with good things so that your youth is renewed like the eagle's."

Notes:

_____

_____

_____

_____

_____

_____

_____

_____

_____

I thank You, God, that...

You forgive me!

For Your Word says in Psalm 103:12,

"As far as the east is from the west, so far has he removed our transgressions from us."

Notes:

_____

_____

_____

_____

_____

_____

_____

_____

_____

I thank You, God, that...

My heart rejoices!

For Your Word says in Psalm 105:3,

"Glory in his holy name, let the hearts of those who seek the Lord rejoice."

Notes:

_____

_____

_____

_____

_____

_____

_____

_____

_____

I thank You, God, that...

You love me forever!

For Your Word says in Psalm 106:1,

"Give thanks to the Lord, for he is good, his love endures forever."

Notes:

_____

_____

_____

_____

_____

_____

_____

_____

_____

I thank You, God, that...

I can rejoice every day!

For Your Word says in Psalm 118:24–26,

"The Lord has done it this very day, let us rejoice today and be glad. Lord save us! Lord grant us success! Blessed is he who comes in the name of the Lord. From the house of the Lord, we bless you."

Notes:

_____

_____

_____

_____

_____

_____

_____

_____

_____

I thank You, God, that...

My help comes from You!

For Your Word says in Psalm 121:1–2,

"I lift my eyes to the mountains, where does my help come from? My help comes from the Lord, the Maker of heaven and earth."

Notes:

_____

_____

_____

_____

_____

_____

_____

_____

_____

I thank You, God, that...

I am fearfully and wonderfully made!

For Your Word says in Psalm 139:13–14,

"For you created my inmost being, you knit me together in my mother's womb. I praise you because I am fearfully and wonderfully made, your works are wonderful, I know that full well."

Notes:

_____

_____

_____

_____

_____

_____

_____

_____

I thank You, God, that...
I will praise You all my life!
For Your Word says in Psalm 146:2,
"I will praise the Lord all my life, I will sing praise to my God as long as I live."

Notes:

_____

_____

_____

_____

_____

_____

_____

_____

_____

I thank You, God, that...

I am successful!

For Your Word says in Proverbs 2:7,

"He holds success in store for the upright, he is a shield to those whose walk is blameless."

Notes:

_____

_____

_____

_____

_____

_____

_____

_____

_____

I thank You, God, that...

You give me wisdom and knowledge!

For Your Word says in Proverbs 2:10,

"For wisdom will enter your heart, and knowledge will be pleasant to your soul."

Notes:

_____

_____

_____

_____

_____

_____

_____

_____

I thank You, God, that...
You give me discretion and understanding!
For Your Word says in Proverbs 2:11,
"Discretion will protect you, and understanding will guard you."

Notes:

_____

_____

_____

_____

_____

_____

_____

_____

I thank You, God, that...

You make my paths straight!

For Your Word says in Proverbs 3:5–6,

"Trust in the Lord with all your heart and lean not on your own understanding, in all your ways submit to him, and he will make your paths straight."

Notes:

_____

_____

_____

_____

_____

_____

_____

_____

_____

I thank You, God, that...
I have wisdom and understanding!
For Your Word says in Proverbs 3:13–14,
"Blessed are those who find wisdom, those who gain understanding, for she is more profitable than silver and yields better returns than gold."

Notes:

_____

_____

_____

_____

_____

_____

_____

_____

_____

I thank You, God, that...
I will live a long life!
For Your Word says in Proverbs 13:3,
"Those who guard their lips preserve their lives, but those who speak rashly will come to ruin."

Notes:

_____

_____

_____

_____

_____

_____

_____

_____

I thank You, God, that...

My plans are successful!

For Your Word says in Proverbs 16:3,

"Commit your plans to the Lord and they will succeed."

Notes:

_____

_____

_____

_____

_____

_____

_____

_____

_____

I thank You, God, that...
I only speak life-giving words!
For Your Word says in Proverbs 18:21,
"The tongue has the power of life and death, and those who love it will eat its fruit."

Notes:

_____

_____

_____

_____

_____

_____

_____

_____

_____

I thank You, God, that...

I am a truthful witness!

For Your Word says in Proverbs 19:5,

"A false witness will not go unpunished, and whoever pours out lies will not go free."

Notes:

_____

_____

_____

_____

_____

_____

_____

_____

_____

I thank You, God, that...
I speak positive words over myself daily!
For Your Word says in Proverbs 23:7,
"As a man thinks in his heart, so is he."

Notes:

_____

_____

_____

_____

_____

_____

_____

_____

_____

I thank You, God, that...

I am a beautiful and priceless treasure!

For Your Word says in Ecclesiastes 3:11,

"He has made everything beautiful in its time. He has also set eternity in the human heart, yet no one can fathom what God has done from beginning to end."

Notes:

_____

_____

_____

_____

_____

_____

_____

_____

I thank You, God, that...

I am strong and powerful!

For Your Word says in Isaiah 40:29,

"He gives strength to the weary and increases the power of the weak."

Notes:

_____

_____

_____

_____

_____

_____

_____

_____

_____

I thank You, God, that...

My hope is in You!

For Your Word says in Isaiah 40:31,

"But those who hope in the Lord will renew their strength. They will soar on wings like eagles, they will run and not grow weary, they will walk and not be faint."

Notes:

_____

_____

_____

_____

_____

_____

_____

_____

_____

I thank You, God, that...

You have chosen me!

For Your Word says in Isaiah 41:9,

"I took you from the ends of the earth, from its farthest corners I called you. I said, 'You are my servant'; I have chosen you and have not rejected you."

Notes:

_____

_____

_____

_____

_____

_____

_____

_____

_____

_____

I thank You, God, that...

You are with me!

For Your Word says in Isaiah 41:10,

"So do not fear, for I am with you; do not be dismayed, for I am your God. I will strengthen you and help you; I will uphold you with my righteous right hand."

Notes:

_____

_____

_____

_____

_____

_____

_____

_____

_____

I thank You, God, that...

You help me!

For Your Word says in Isaiah 41:13,

"For I am the Lord your God who takes hold of your right hand and says to you, do not fear, I will help you."

Notes:

_____

_____

_____

_____

_____

_____

_____

_____

_____

I thank You, God, that...

I am precious in Your sight!

For Your Word says in Isaiah 43:4,

"Since you are precious and honored in my site, and because I love you, I will give people in exchange for you, nations in exchange for your life."

Notes:

_____

_____

_____

_____

_____

_____

_____

_____

I thank You, God, that...

You sustain me!

For Your Word says in Isaiah 46:4,

"Even to your old age and gray hairs, I am he, I am he who will sustain you. I have made you and I will carry you; I will sustain you and I will rescue you."

Notes:

_____

_____

_____

_____

_____

_____

_____

_____

_____

I thank You, God, that...
You always remember me!
For Your Word says in Isaiah 49:16,
"See, I have engraved you on the palms of my hands; your walls are ever before me."

Notes:

_____

_____

_____

_____

_____

_____

_____

I thank You, God, that...

I am healed!

For Your Word says in Isaiah 53:5,

"But he was pierced for our transgressions, he was crushed for our iniquities; the punishment that bought us peace was on him, and by his wounds we are healed."

Notes:

_____

_____

_____

_____

_____

_____

_____

_____

_____

I thank You, God, that...

Nothing can beat me!

For Your Word says in Isaiah 54:17,

"'No weapon formed against you will prevail, and you will refute every tongue that accuses you. This is the heritage of the servants of the Lord, and this is their vindication from me,' declares the Lord."

Notes:

_____

_____

_____

_____

_____

_____

_____

_____

I thank You, God, that...

You have set me apart!

For Your Word says in Jeremiah 1:5,

"Before I formed you in the womb I knew you, before you were born
I set you apart; I appointed you as a prophet to the nations."

Notes:

_____

_____

_____

_____

_____

_____

_____

_____

I thank You, God, that...

No one can overcome me!

For Your Word says in Jeremiah 1:19,

"'They will fight against you but will not overcome you, for I am with you and will rescue you,' declares the Lord."

Notes:

_____

_____

_____

_____

_____

_____

_____

_____

I thank You, God, that...

I am blessed because I trust in You!

For Your Word says in Jeremiah 17:7,

"But blessed is the one who trusts in the Lord, whose confidence is in Him."

Notes:

_____

_____

_____

_____

_____

_____

_____

_____

I thank You, God, that...

You are with me!

For Your Word says in Jeremiah 20:11,

"But the Lord is with me like a mighty warrior so that my persecutors will stumble and not prevail. They will fail and be thoroughly disgraced; their dishonor will never be forgotten."

Notes:

_____

_____

_____

_____

_____

_____

_____

_____

_____

I thank You, God, that...

I have a prosperous and hopeful future!

For Your Word says in Jeremiah 29:11,

"'For I know the plans I have for you,' declares the Lord, 'plans to prosper you and not to harm you, plans to give you hope and a future.'"

Notes:

_____

_____

_____

_____

_____

_____

_____

_____

_____

I thank You, God, that...
I sought You and have found You!
For Your Word says in Jeremiah 29:13,
"You will seek me and find me when you seek me with your whole heart."

Notes:

_____

_____

_____

_____

_____

_____

_____

_____

I thank You, God, that...

Nothing is too hard for You!

For Your Word says in Jeremiah 32:27,

"I am the Lord, the God of all mankind. Is anything too hard for me?"

Notes:

_____

_____

_____

_____

_____

_____

_____

_____

I thank You, God, that...
I shine like the stars!
For Your Word says in Daniel 12:3,
"Those who are wise will shine like the brightness of the heavens, and those who lead many to righteousness, like the stars forever and ever."

Notes:

_____

_____

_____

_____

_____

_____

_____

_____

I thank You, God, that...

My jubilee has come!

For Your Word says in Joel 2:25–26,

> I will repay you for the years the locusts have eaten, the great locust and the young locust, the other locusts and the locust swarm, my great army that I send among you. You will have plenty to eat until you are full, and you will praise the name of the Lord your God, who has worked wonders for you, never again will my people be shamed.

Notes:

_____

_____

_____

_____

_____

_____

_____

_____

I thank You, God, that...

Salvation comes from You!

For Your Word says in Jonah 2:9,

"But I with shouts of grateful praise, will sacrifice to you. What I have vowed I will make good. I will say, 'Salvation comes from the Lord.'"

Notes:

_____

_____

_____

_____

_____

_____

_____

_____

I thank You, God, that...

You show me what You require!

For Your Word says in Micah 6:8,

"He has shown you, O mortal, what is good. And what does the Lord require of you? To act justly and to love mercy, and to walk humbly with your God."

Notes:

_____

_____

_____

_____

_____

_____

_____

_____

_____

I thank You, God, that...

You give me honor and praise!

For Your Word says in Zephaniah 3:20,

"'At that time, I will gather you, at that time I will bring you home. I will give you honor and praise among all the peoples of the earth when I restore your fortunes before your eyes,' says the Lord."

Notes:

_____

_____

_____

_____

_____

_____

_____

_____

_____

I thank You, God, that...

I am extremely blessed!

For Your Word says in Matthew 5:3–11,

> Blessed are the poor in spirit, for theirs is the kingdom of heaven. Blessed are those who mourn, for they will be comforted. Blessed are the meek, for they will inherit the earth. Blessed are those who hunger and thirst for righteousness, for they will be filled. Blessed are the merciful, for they will be shown mercy. Blessed are the pure in heart, for they will see God. Blessed are the peacemakers, for they will be called children of God. Blessed are those who are persecuted because of righteousness, for theirs is the kingdom of heaven. Blessed are you when people insult you, persecute you and falsely say all kinds of evil against you because of me.

Notes:

_____

_____

_____

_____

_____

_____

_____

_____

I thank You, God, that...
I let my light shine!
For Your Word says in Matthew 5:16,
"Let your light shine before men, that they may see your good works and glorify your Father which is in heaven."

Notes:

_____

_____

_____

_____

_____

_____

_____

_____

_____

I thank You, God, that...
I will not worry about anything!
For Your Word says in Matthew 6:27,
"Can any one of you by worrying add a single hour to your life?"

Notes:

_____

_____

_____

_____

_____

_____

_____

_____

I thank You, God, that...

I will not worry about tomorrow!

For Your Word says in Matthew 6:34,

"Therefore, do not worry about tomorrow, for tomorrow will worry about itself. Each day has enough trouble of its own."

Notes:

_____

_____

_____

_____

_____

_____

_____

_____

_____

I thank You, God, that...

You give me rest!

For Your Word says in Matthew 11:28–30,

"Come to me, all of you who are weary and burdened, and I will give you rest. Take my yoke upon you and learn from me, for I am gentle and humble in heart, and you will find rest for your souls. For my yoke is easy and my burden is light."

Notes:

_____

_____

_____

_____

_____

_____

_____

_____

_____

I thank You, God, that...

I can move mountains!

For Your Word says in Matthew 17:20,

"Truly I tell you, if you have faith as small as a mustard seed, you can say to this mountain 'Move from here to there,' and it will move. Nothing will be impossible for you."

Notes:

_____

_____

_____

_____

_____

_____

_____

_____

_____

I thank You, God, that...
I love You with all my being!
For Your Word says in Matthew 22:37,
"Jesus replied: 'Love the Lord with all your heart and with all your soul and with all your mind.'"

Notes:

_____

_____

_____

_____

_____

_____

_____

_____

I thank You, God, that...

I am exalted!

For Your Word says in Matthew 23:12,

"For those who exalt themselves will be humbled, and those who humble themselves will be exalted."

Notes:

_____

_____

_____

_____

_____

_____

_____

_____

_____

I thank You, God, that...

I am ready!

For Your Word says in Matthew 24:44,

"So, you must be ready because the Son of Man will come at an hour when you do not expect him."

Notes:

_____

_____

_____

_____

_____

_____

_____

_____

I thank You, God, that...
I believe that I can do anything!
For Your Word says in Mark 9:23,
"'If you can?' said Jesus. 'Everything is possible to him who believes.'"

Notes:

_____

_____

_____

_____

_____

_____

_____

_____

_____

I thank You, God, that...

I receive what I ask for in prayer!

For Your Word says in Mark 11:24,

"Therefore, I tell you, whatever you ask for in prayer, believe that you have received it, and it will be yours."

Notes:

_____

_____

_____

_____

_____

_____

_____

_____

I thank You, God, that...

I am healthy!

For Your Word says in Luke 5:31,

"Jesus answered them, 'It is not the healthy who need a doctor, but the sick.'"

Notes:

_____

_____

_____

_____

_____

_____

_____

_____

_____

I thank You, God, that...
I forgive myself and others!
For Your Word says in Luke 6:37,
"Do not judge others, and you will not be judged. Do not condemn, and you will not be condemned. Forgive, and you will be forgiven."

Notes:

_____

_____

_____

_____

_____

_____

_____

_____

_____

I thank You, God, that...

I am an overcomer!

For Your Word says in Luke 10:19,

"I have given you authority to trample on snakes and scorpions and to overcome all the power of the enemy, nothing will harm you."

Notes:

_____

_____

_____

_____

_____

_____

_____

_____

I thank You, God, that...

I love You and my neighbor!

For Your Word says in Luke 10:27,

"He answered, 'Love the Lord your God with all your heart and with all your soul and with all your strength and with all your mind'; and 'Love your neighbor as yourself.'"

Notes:

_____

_____

_____

_____

_____

_____

_____

_____

_____

I thank You, God, that...

I am worth more!

For Your Word says in Luke 12:7,

"Indeed, the very hairs on your head are numbered. Don't be afraid, you are worth more than many sparrows."

Notes:

_____

_____

_____

_____

_____

_____

_____

_____

I thank You, God, that...

I am valuable!

For Your Word says in Luke 12:24,

"Consider the ravens: They do not sow or reap; they have no storeroom or barn, yet God feeds them. And how much more valuable you are than birds!"

Notes:

_____

_____

_____

_____

_____

_____

_____

_____

_____

I thank You, God, that...

I am a warrior, not a worrier!

For Your Word says in Luke 12:25,

"Who of you by worrying can add a single hour to your life?"

Notes:

_____

_____

_____

_____

_____

_____

_____

_____

I thank You, God, that...
My treasure is with You!
For Your Word says in Luke 12:34,
"For where your treasure is, there your heart will be also."

Notes:

_____

_____

_____

_____

_____

_____

_____

_____

I thank You, God, that...

All things are possible with You!

For Your Word says in Luke 18:27,

"Jesus replied, 'What is impossible with man is possible with God.'"

Notes:

_____

_____

_____

_____

_____

_____

_____

_____

_____

I thank You, God, that...
You have found me!
For Your Word says in Luke 19:10,
"For the Son of Man came to seek and save the lost."

Notes:

_____

_____

_____

_____

_____

_____

_____

_____

_____

I thank You, God, that...

I am Your child!

For Your Word says in John 1:12,

"Yet to all who did receive him, to those who believed in his name, he gave the right to become children of God."

Notes:

_____

_____

_____

_____

_____

_____

_____

_____

I thank You, God, that...

You love me so much!

For Your Word says in John 3:16,

"For God so loved the world that He gave His only begotten Son, that whoever believes in Him should not perish but have everlasting life."

Notes:

_____

_____

_____

_____

_____

_____

_____

_____

_____

I thank You, God, that...
I will never be thirsty!
For Your Word says in John 4:13–14,
"Whoever drinks the water I give them will never thirst. Indeed, the water I give them will become in them a spring of water welling up to eternal life."

Notes:

_____

_____

_____

_____

_____

_____

_____

_____

_____

I thank You, God, that...

I will never be hungry or thirsty!

For Your Word says in John 6:35,

"Then Jesus declared, 'I am the bread of life. Whoever comes to me will never go never hungry, whoever believes in me will never be thirsty.'"

Notes:

_____

_____

_____

_____

_____

_____

_____

_____

_____

I thank You, God, that...

I am set free!

For Your Word says in John 8:31–32,

"To the Jews who had believed him, Jesus said, 'If you hold to my teaching, you really are my disciples. Then you will know the truth, and the truth will set you free.'"

Notes:

_____

_____

_____

_____

_____

_____

_____

_____

I thank You, God, that...

I produce much fruit!

For Your Word says in John 15:5,

"I am the vine; you are the branches. If you remain in me and I in you, you will bear much fruit, apart from me you can to nothing."

Notes:

_____

_____

_____

_____

_____

_____

_____

_____

_____

I thank You, God, that...

I am a friend of God!

For Your Word says in John 15:14–15,

"You are my friends if you do what I command. I no longer call you servants, because a servant does not know his master's business. Instead, I have called you friends, for everything I learned from my Father I have made known to you."

Notes:

_____

_____

_____

_____

_____

_____

_____

_____

_____

I thank You, God, that...

I am filled with Your joy!

For Your Word says in John 17:13,

"I am coming to you now, but I say these things while I am still in the world, so that they may have the full measure of my joy within them."

Notes:

_____

_____

_____

_____

_____

_____

_____

_____

I thank You, God, that...

I am one with Christ!

For Your Word says in John 17:20–21,

"My prayer is not for them alone. I pray also for those who believe in me through their message, that all of them may be one, Father, just as you are in me, and I am in you. May they also be in us so that the world may believe that you have sent me."

Notes:

_____

_____

_____

_____

_____

_____

_____

_____

I thank You, God, that...

Your power brings salvation!

For Your Word says in Romans 1:16,

"For I am not ashamed of the gospel, because it is the power of God that brings salvation to everyone who believes: first to the Jew, then to the Gentile."

Notes:

_____

_____

_____

_____

_____

_____

_____

_____

_____

I thank You, God, that...
You give me righteousness through faith!
For Your Word says in Romans 3:22,
"This righteousness is given through faith in Jesus Christ to all who believe. There is no difference between Jew and Gentile."

Notes:

_____

_____

_____

_____

_____

_____

_____

_____

_____

I thank You, God, that...

I am free!

For Your Word says in Romans 8:1–2,

"Therefore, there is now no condemnation for those who are in Christ Jesus, because through Christ Jesus the law of the Spirit who gives life has set you free from the law of sin and death."

Notes:

_____

_____

_____

_____

_____

_____

_____

_____

_____

I thank You, God, that...

I am Your child!

For Your Word says in Romans 8:14,

"For those who are led by the spirit of God are the children of God."

Notes:

_____

_____

_____

_____

_____

_____

_____

_____

_____

I thank You, God, that...

I am a joint heir with Christ!

For Your Word says in Romans 8:16–17,

"The Spirit himself testifies with our spirit that we are God's children. Now if we are children, then we are heirs, heirs of God and co-heirs with Christ, if indeed, we share in his sufferings in order that we may also share in his glory."

Notes:

_____

_____

_____

_____

_____

_____

_____

_____

_____

I thank You, God, that...
My joy is here!
For Your Word says in Romans 8:18,
"For I consider that the sufferings of this present time are not worthy to be compared with the glory which shall be revealed in us."

Notes:

_____

_____

_____

_____

_____

_____

_____

_____

_____

THANK YOU, GOD

I thank You, God, that...

You work everything for my good!

For Your Word says in Romans 8:28,

"And we know that in all things God works for the good of those who love him, and have been called according to his purpose."

Notes:

_____

_____

_____

_____

_____

_____

_____

_____

I thank You, God, that...

You are for me!

For Your Word says in Romans 8:31,

"If God be for us, who can be against us?"

Notes:

_____

_____

_____

_____

_____

_____

_____

_____

I thank You, God, that...

I am more than a conqueror!

For Your Word says in Romans 8:37,

"No, in all these things, we are more than conquerors through him who loved us."

Notes:

_____

_____

_____

_____

_____

_____

_____

_____

_____

I thank You, God, that...

I am saved!

For Your Word says in Romans 10:9–10,

"If you declare with your mouth, 'Jesus is Lord,' and you believe in your heart God raised him from the dead, you will be saved. For it is with your heart you believe and are justified, and it is with your mouth that you profess your faith and are saved."

Notes:

_____

_____

_____

_____

_____

_____

_____

_____

_____

I thank You, God, that...

My mind is renewed!

For Your Word says in Romans 12:2,

"Do not conform to the pattern of this world but be transformed by the renewing of your mind. Then you will be able to test and approve what God's will is, his good, pleasing, and perfect will."

Notes:

_____

_____

_____

_____

_____

_____

_____

_____

_____

I thank You, God, that...
I am accepted by Christ!
For Your Word says in Romans 15:7,
"Accept one another, then, just as Christ accepted you, to bring praise to God."

Notes:

_____

_____

_____

_____

_____

_____

_____

_____

_____

I thank You, God, that...

You give me wisdom!

For Your Word says in 1 Corinthians 1:30,

"It is because of him that you are in Christ Jesus, who has become for us wisdom from God—that is, our righteousness, holiness, and redemption."

Notes:

_____

_____

_____

_____

_____

_____

_____

_____

_____

_____

I thank You, God, that...
I have the mind of Christ!
For Your Word says in 1 Corinthians 2:16,
"'Who has known the mind of the Lord so as to instruct him?' But we have the mind of Christ."

Notes:

_____

_____

_____

_____

_____

_____

_____

_____

_____

I thank You, God, that...

I am patient and kind!

For Your Word says in 1 Corinthians 13:4–8,

> Love is patient, love is kind. It does not envy, it does not boast, it is not proud. It is not rude, it is not self-seeking, it is not easily angered, it keeps no record of wrongs. Love does not delight in evil but rejoices with the truth. It always protects, always trusts, always hopes, always perseveres. Love never fails.

Notes:

_____

_____

_____

_____

_____

_____

_____

_____

_____

I thank You, God, that...

You are the God of peace!

For Your Word says in 1 Corinthians 14:33,

"For God is not a God of disorder but of peace, as in all the congregations of the Lord's people."

Notes:

_____

_____

_____

_____

_____

_____

_____

_____

I thank You, God, that...

I am gifted!

For Your Word says in 1 Corinthians 14:37,

"If anyone thinks they are a prophet or otherwise gifted by the Spirit, let them acknowledge that what I am writing to you is the Lord's command."

Notes:

_____

_____

_____

_____

_____

_____

_____

_____

_____

I thank You, God, that...

I have victory through Christ!

For Your Word says in 1 Corinthians 15:57,

"But thanks be to God! He gives us the victory through our Lord Jesus Christ."

Notes:

_____

_____

_____

_____

_____

_____

_____

_____

I thank You, God, that...

All your promises are *yes* and *amen*!

For Your Word says in 2 Corinthians 1:20,

"For no matter how many promises God has made, they are 'Yes' in Christ. And so through him the 'Amen' is spoken by us to the glory of God."

Notes:

_____

_____

_____

_____

_____

_____

_____

_____

_____

I thank You, God, that...

I am anointed!

For Your Word says in 2 Corinthians 1:21–22,

"Now it is God who makes both us and you stand firm in Christ. He anointed us, set his seal of ownership on us, and put his Spirit in our hearts as a deposit, guaranteeing what is to come."

Notes:

_____

_____

_____

_____

_____

_____

_____

_____

_____

I thank You, God, that...

My body is a temple of the Holy Spirit!

For Your Word says in 1 Corinthians 6–19,

"Do you not know that your bodies are temples of the Holy Spirit, who is in you, whom you have received from God?"

Notes:

_____

_____

_____

_____

_____

_____

_____

_____

_____

I thank You, God, that...

I am bold!

For Your Word says in 2 Corinthians 3:12,

"Therefore, since we have such hope, we are very bold."

Notes:

_____

_____

_____

_____

_____

_____

_____

_____

_____

I thank You, God, that...

I am transformed!

For Your Word says in 2 Corinthians 3:18,

"And we all, who with unveiled faces contemplate the Lord's glory, are being transformed into his image with ever-increasing glory, which comes from the Lord, who is the spirit."

Notes:

_____

_____

_____

_____

_____

_____

_____

_____

_____

I thank You, God, that...

I am a new creation!

For Your Word says in 2 Corinthians 5:17,

"Therefore, if anyone is in Christ, the new creation has come. The old has gone, the new is here."

Notes:

_____

_____

_____

_____

_____

_____

_____

_____

_____

I thank You, God, that...
I am abundantly blessed!
For Your Word says in 2 Corinthians 9:8,
"And God is able to bless you abundantly, so that in all things at all times, having all that you need to abound in every good work."

Notes:

_____

_____

_____

_____

_____

_____

_____

_____

_____

I thank You, God, that...

I take every thought captive!

For Your Word says in 2 Corinthians 10:5,

"We demolish arguments and every pretension that sets itself up against the knowledge of God, and we take every thought captive to make it obedient to Christ."

Notes:

_____

_____

_____

_____

_____

_____

_____

_____

_____

I thank You, God, that...

Your grace is sufficient!

For Your Word says in 2 Corinthians 12:9,

"But he said to me, 'My grace is sufficient for you, for my power is made perfect in weakness.'"

Notes:

_____

_____

_____

_____

_____

_____

_____

_____

I thank You, God, that...

I am redeemed!

For Your Word says in Galatians 3:13,

"Christ redeemed us from the curse of the law by becoming a curse for us, for it is written: 'Cursed is everyone who is hung on a pole.'"

Notes:

_____

_____

_____

_____

_____

_____

_____

_____

_____

_____

I thank You, God, that...

I am a child of the Heavenly Father!

For Your Word says in Galatians 4:4–7,

> But when the set time had fully come, God sent his Son,
> born of a woman, born under the law, to redeem those
> under the law, that we might receive adoption to sonship.
> Because you are His sons, God sent the spirit of his Son
> into our hearts, the Spirit who calls out, "Abba, Father."
> So, you are no longer a slave but God's child; and since
> you are his child, God has made you also an heir.

Notes:

_____

_____

_____

_____

_____

_____

_____

_____

I thank You, God, that...

I am free!

For Your Word says in Galatians 5:13,

"You, my brothers and sisters, were called to be free. But do not use your freedom to indulge in the flesh, rather, serve one another humbly in love."

Notes:

_____

_____

_____

_____

_____

_____

_____

_____

_____

I thank You, God, that...

I am aware!

For Your Word says in Galatians 6:7,

"Do not be deceived: God cannot be mocked. A man reaps what he sows."

Notes:

_____

_____

_____

_____

_____

_____

_____

_____

I thank You, God, that...
I will reap a harvest!
For Your Word says in Galatians 6:9,
"Let us not become weary in doing good, for at the proper time we will reap a harvest if we do not give up."

Notes:

_____

_____

_____

_____

_____

_____

_____

_____

I thank You, God, that...

I am blessed with every spiritual blessing!

For Your Word says in Ephesians 1:3,

"Praise be to the God and Father of our Lord Jesus Christ, who has blessed us in the heavenly realms with every spiritual blessing in Christ."

Notes:

_____

_____

_____

_____

_____

_____

_____

_____

_____

I thank You, God, that...

I have been saved by grace!

For Your Word says in Ephesians 2:8–9,

"For it is by grace you have been saved through faith—and this is not from yourselves, it is the gift of God—not by works, so that no one can boast."

Notes:

_____

_____

_____

_____

_____

_____

_____

_____

_____

I thank You, God, that...

I am created to do good works!

For Your Word says in Ephesians 2:10,

"For we are God's handiwork, created in Christ Jesus to do good works, which God prepared in advance for us to do."

Notes:

_____

_____

_____

_____

_____

_____

_____

_____

_____

I thank You, God, that...

You do more than I ask!

For Your Word says in Ephesians 3:20–21,

"Now to him who can do immeasurably more than all we ask or imagine, according to his power that at work within us, to him be glory in the church and in Christ Jesus through all generations forever and ever! Amen."

Notes:

_____

_____

_____

_____

_____

_____

_____

_____

_____

I thank You, God, that...
I am humble and gentle!
For Your Word says in Ephesians 4:2,
"Be completely humble and gentle, be patient, bearing with one another in love."

Notes:

_____

_____

_____

_____

_____

_____

_____

_____

_____

I thank You, God, that...

I build others up!

For Your Word says in Ephesians 4:29,

"Do not let any unwholesome talk come out of your mouths, but only what is helpful for building others up according to their needs, that it may benefit those who listen."

Notes:

_____

_____

_____

_____

_____

_____

_____

_____

_____

I thank You, God, that...

For Your good work in me!

For Your Word says in Philippians 1:6,

"Being confident of this, that he began a good work in you will carry it on to completion until the day of Christ Jesus."

Notes:

_____

_____

_____

_____

_____

_____

_____

_____

I thank You, God, that...

Your peace guards my heart!

For Your Word says in Philippians 4:6–7,

"Do not be anxious about anything, but in every situation, by prayer and petition, with thanksgiving, present your requests to God. And the peace of God, which transcends all understanding, will guard your hearts and minds in Christ Jesus."

Notes:

_____

_____

_____

_____

_____

_____

_____

_____

I thank You, God, that...

I think positive thoughts!

For Your Word says in Philippians 4:8,

"Finally, brothers and sisters, whatever is true, whatever is noble, whatever is right, whatever is pure, whatever is lovely, whatever is admirable, if anything is excellent or praiseworthy, think about such things."

Notes:

_____

_____

_____

_____

_____

_____

_____

_____

I thank You, God, that...
I have removed the words *I can't* from my mind!
For Your Word says in Philippians 4:13,
"I can do *all things* through Christ who strengthens me."

Notes:

_____

_____

_____

_____

_____

_____

_____

_____

I thank You, God, that...
I lack nothing!
For Your Word says in Philippians 4:19,
"My God will supply all your needs according to His riches and glory
in Christ Jesus."

Notes:

_____

_____

_____

_____

_____

_____

_____

_____

I thank You, God, that...

I am encouraged!

For Your Word says in Colossians 2:2,

"My goal is that they may be encouraged in heart and united in love, so that they may have the full riches of complete understanding, in order that they may know the mystery of God, namely, Christ."

Notes:

_____

_____

_____

_____

_____

_____

_____

_____

I thank You, God, that...

I am overflowing with joy and thankfulness!

For Your Word says in Colossians 2:6–7,

"So then, just as you received Christ Jesus as Lord, continue to live your lives in him, rooted and built up in him, strengthened in your faith as you were taught and overflowing with thankfulness."

Notes:

_____

_____

_____

_____

_____

_____

_____

_____

_____

I thank You, God, that...

I am complete in Christ!

For Your Word says in Colossians 2:9–10,

"For in Christ all the fullness of the Deity lives in bodily form, and in Christ you have been brought to fullness."

Notes:

_____

_____

_____

_____

_____

_____

_____

_____

_____

I thank You, God, that...

Christ is my life!

For Your Word says in Colossians 3:4,

"When Christ, who is your life, appears, then you also will appear with him in glory."

Notes:

_____

_____

_____

_____

_____

_____

_____

_____

_____

_____

I thank You, God, that...

I am chosen by You!

For Your Word says in Colossians 3:12,

"Therefore, as God's chosen people, holy and dearly loved, clothe yourselves with compassion, kindness, humility, gentleness, and patience."

Notes:

_____

_____

_____

_____

_____

_____

_____

_____

I thank You, God, that...

I am a forgiver!

For Your Word says in Colossians 3:13,

"Bear with each other and forgive one another if any of you has a grievance against someone. Forgive as the Lord forgave you."

Notes:

_____

_____

_____

_____

_____

_____

_____

_____

I thank You, God, that...

I have the message of Christ!

For Your Word says in Colossians 3:16,

"Let the message of Christ dwell among you richly as you teach and admonish one another with all wisdom through psalms, hymns, and songs from the Spirit, singing to God with gratitude in your hearts."

Notes:

_____

_____

_____

_____

_____

_____

_____

_____

I thank You, God, that...

I am a hearer and doer of Your Word!

For Your Word says in 1 Timothy 4:16,

"Watch your life and doctrine closely. Persevere in them, because if you do, you will save yourself and your hearers."

Notes:

_____

_____

_____

_____

_____

_____

_____

_____

_____

I thank You, God, that...

Fear cannot touch me!

For Your Word says in 2 Timothy 1:7,

"For I have not given you a spirit of fear, but power, love, and a sound mind."

Notes:

_____

_____

_____

_____

_____

_____

_____

_____

I thank You, God, that...

I am called by You!

For Your Word says in 2 Timothy 1:9,

"He has saved us and called us to a holy life—not because of anything we have done but because of his own purpose and grace."

Notes:

_____

_____

_____

_____

_____

_____

_____

_____

I thank You, God, that...

I am prepared!

For Your Word says in 2 Timothy 4:2,

"Preach the word; be prepared in season and out of season, correct, rebuke, and encourage—with great patience and careful instruction."

Notes:

_____

_____

_____

_____

_____

_____

_____

_____

_____

I thank You, God, that...

I am chosen!

For Your Word says in 1 Thessalonians 1:4,

"For we know, brothers and sisters loved by God, that he has chosen you."

Notes:

_____

_____

_____

_____

_____

_____

_____

_____

_____

I thank You, God, that...

I will be with You forever when You return!

For Your Word says in 1 Thessalonians 4:17–18,

"After that, we who are still alive and are left will be caught up with them together in the clouds to meet the Lord in the air. And so, we will be with the Lord forever. Therefore encourage one another with these words."

Notes:

_____

_____

_____

_____

_____

_____

_____

_____

I thank You, God, that...

I am a doer of Your will!

For Your Word says in 1 Thessalonians 5:16–18,

"Rejoice always, pray continually, give thanks in all circumstances, for this is God's will for you in Christ Jesus."

Notes:

_____

_____

_____

_____

_____

_____

_____

_____

I thank You, God, that...

I am worthy!

For Your Word says in 2 Thessalonians 1:5,

"All this is evidence that God's judgment is right, and as a result you will be counted worthy of the kingdom of God, for which you are suffering."

Notes:

_____

_____

_____

_____

_____

_____

_____

_____

_____

I thank You, God, that...
You direct my heart!
For Your Word says in 2 Thessalonians 3:5,
"May the Lord direct your hearts into God's love and Christ's perseverance."

Notes:

_____

_____

_____

_____

_____

_____

_____

_____

_____

I thank You, God, that...

You have forgiven my sins!

For Your Word says in Hebrews 9:22,

"In fact, the law requires that nearly everything be cleansed with blood, and without the shedding of blood there is no forgiveness."

Notes:

_____

_____

_____

_____

_____

_____

_____

_____

I thank You, God, that...

My eyes are fixed on Jesus!

For Your Word says in Hebrews 12:1–2,

"Therefore, since we are surrounded by such a great cloud of witnesses, let us throw off everything that hinders and the sin that so easily entangles. And let us fix our eyes on Jesus, the author and perfecter of our faith."

Notes:

_____

_____

_____

_____

_____

_____

_____

_____

_____

I thank You, God, that...
I am consumed by You!
For Your Word says in Hebrews 12:29,
"For our God is a consuming fire."

Notes:

_____

_____

_____

_____

_____

_____

_____

_____

I thank You, God, that...

You are always with me!

For Your Word says in Hebrews 13:5,

"Keep your lives free from the love of money and be content with what you have because God has said, 'Never will I leave you; never will I forsake you.'"

Notes:

_____

_____

_____

_____

_____

_____

_____

_____

_____

I thank You, God, that...

I have perseverance!

For Your Word says in James 1:2–3,

"Consider it pure joy, my brothers and sisters, whenever you face trials of many kinds, because you know that the testing of your faith produces perseverance."

Notes:

_____

_____

_____

_____

_____

_____

_____

_____

_____

I thank You, God, that...

I have wisdom!

For Your Word says in James 1:5,

"If any of you lacks wisdom, you should ask God, who gives generously to all without finding fault, and it will be given to you."

Notes:

_____

_____

_____

_____

_____

_____

_____

_____

_____

I thank You, God, that...

The devil cannot come near me!

For Your Word says in James 4:7,

"Submit yourselves, then, to God. Resist the devil and he will flee from you."

Notes:

_____

_____

_____

_____

_____

_____

_____

_____

_____

I thank You, God, that...

You draw near to me!

For Your Word says in James 4:8,

"Come near to God and he will come near to you. Wash your hands you sinners, and purify your hearts, you double-minded."

Notes:

_____

_____

_____

_____

_____

_____

_____

_____

_____

I thank You, God, that...

I am happy!

For Your Word says in James 5:13,

"Is anyone among you in trouble? Let them pray. If anyone is happy? Let them sing songs of praise."

Notes:

_____

_____

_____

_____

_____

_____

_____

I thank You, God, that...

I belong to You!

For Your Word says in 1 Peter 2:9,

"But you are a chosen people, a royal priesthood, a holy nation, God's special possession, that you may declare the praises of him who called you out of darkness into his wonderful light."

Notes:

_____

_____

_____

_____

_____

_____

_____

_____

I thank You, God, that...

I have been healed!

For Your Word says in 1 Peter 2:24,

"He himself bore our sins in his body on the cross, so that we might die to sins and live for righteousness; 'by his wounds you have been healed.'"

Notes:

_____

_____

_____

_____

_____

_____

_____

_____

_____

_____

I thank You, God, that...
I am righteous and forgiven!
For Your Word says in 1 John 1:9,
"If we confess our sins, he is faithful and just and will forgive us our sins and purify us from all unrighteousness."

Notes:

_____

_____

_____

_____

_____

_____

_____

_____

I thank You, God, that...

I am forgiven!

For Your Word says in 1 John 2:12,

"I am writing to you, dear children, because your sins have been forgiven on account of his name."

Notes:

_____

_____

_____

_____

_____

_____

_____

_____

I thank You, God, that...

The anointing from God remains in me!

For Your Word says in 1 John 2:27,

"As for you, the anointing you received from him remains in you, and you do not need anyone to teach you. But as his anointing teaches you about all things and as that anointing is real, not counterfeit—just as it has been taught you, remain in him."

Notes:

_____

_____

_____

_____

_____

_____

_____

_____

_____

I thank You, God, that...

You know me!

For Your Word says in 1 John 3:20,

"If our hearts condemn us, we know that God is greater than our hearts, and he knows everything."

Notes:

_____

_____

_____

_____

_____

_____

_____

_____

_____

I thank You, God, that...

I love others!

For Your Word says in 1 John 4:7,

"Dear friends, let us love one another, for love comes from God. Everyone who loves has been born of God and knows God."

Notes:

_____

_____

_____

_____

_____

_____

_____

_____

_____

I thank You, God, that...
I am loved by Jesus!
For Your Word says in 1 John 4:19,
"We love him because he first loved us."

Notes:

_____

_____

_____

_____

_____

_____

_____

_____

_____

I thank You, God, that...

I am safe!

For Your Word says in 1 John 5:18,

"We know that anyone born of God does not continue to sin, the One who was born of God keeps them safe, and the evil one cannot harm them."

Notes:

_____

_____

_____

_____

_____

_____

_____

_____

_____

_____

I thank You, God, that...
I enjoy good health!
For Your Word says in 3 John 1:2,
"Dear friend, I pray that you may enjoy good health and that all may go well with you, even as your soul is getting along well."

Notes:

_____

_____

_____

_____

_____

_____

_____

_____

I thank You, God, that...

I am triumphant!

For Your Word says in Revelation 12:11,

"They triumphed over him by the blood of the Lamb and by the word of their testimony, they did not love their lives so much as to shrink from death."

Notes:

_____

_____

_____

_____

_____

_____

_____

_____

_____

_____

I thank You, God, that...

I am victorious!

For Your Word says in Revelation 21:7,

"Those who are victorious will inherit all this, and I will be their God and they will be my children."

Notes:

_____

_____

_____

_____

_____

_____

_____

_____

Chapter 3

Positive Thoughts Wall

Have you ever seen a picture online or in a magazine that had encouraging words that just spoke to you? Perhaps you took it and put it up on your refrigerator or somewhere else in your home. If you didn't, you might eventually forget the thought or where you saw it at. I have done that. Speaking positive thoughts to yourself can help to change a bad day into a good day and even put a smile on yourself. It's been said that it takes twenty-one days to form a habit, so I encourage you to speak positive thoughts out loud over yourself every day. You never know how much of a difference it will make in your life until you start doing it.

Creating a Positive Thoughts Wall

The following pages contain positive thoughts that you can speak over yourself and others.

Here are some suggestions for creating a positive thoughts wall.

If you have a computer that has Microsoft Word on it, open Microsoft Word. Create a one-line, one-column table. Go into the table properties inside the table and go to Borders and Shading and select a soft color like a light blue. The first line in the table should say something like "I thank You, God, that..." or "I declare in Jesus' name that..." Below that, select seven of the positive thoughts from the following pages and put them in the table. Center each line and put a space between it. Highlight all lines and select a font such as Arial or Monotype Corsiva and make the font size large enough for all the lines to fill the entire page. Save the document and print it out. Place the document in a prominent place in your home for you and anyone else to see it. If you don't have access to a computer with Microsoft Word, take a plain or colored sheet of paper and write the thoughts on there.

Speak Positive Thoughts Out Loud Daily

I encourage you to read them out loud daily. If there are others in your home, have everyone read the positive thoughts out loud together. Read them as often as needed. You can even post them at work for your coworkers to see them. Even if you or someone else is having a bad day, just saying these thoughts out loud every day can turn the whole day around.

If you know of someone, perhaps a family member, friend, coworker, who is going through a rough time like the loss of a job, an illness, or some other challenge, make a copy of these thoughts to give to them and encourage them to read them out loud daily. Not only will it bless them, but it will bless you as well, knowing that you contributed something positive to help them in their situation. If you have created a positive thoughts wall, show it to them and encourage them to create a positive thoughts wall of their own.

Positive Thought Statements

I am somebody!

I do matter!

I am loved!

I am valuable!

I am significant!

I am courageous!

I am determined!

I am precious!

I am beautiful!

I am unbreakable!

I am unstoppable!

I am anointed!

I am worthy!

I am secure!

I am precious!

I am beautiful!

I am secure!

I am healed!

I am whole!

I am positive!

I am confident!

I am strong!

I am forgiving!

I am grateful!

I am empowered!

I am undefeatable!

I am an overcomer!

I am brave!

I am fearless!

I am bold!

I am strong!

I am healthy!

I am unbreakable!

I am unstoppable!

I am anointed!

I am chosen by God!

I am resourceful!

I am ready!

I am intelligent!

I am highly favored!

I am victorious!

I am important!

I am excited about today!

I am God's masterpiece!

I am made in God's image!

I am victorious in every area of my life!

I am thankful for every day I wake up!

I am a hearer and doer of God's Word!

I am happy!

I am capable!

I am gifted!

I am successful!

I am wealthy!

I am prepared!

I am well-abled!

I am extremely blessed!

I am redeemed!

I am more than a conqueror!

I am empowered to win!

I am a child of God!

I am the head and not the tail!

I am complete in Christ!

I am overflowing with joy!

I am a giant slayer like David!

I am a beautiful and priceless treasure!

I can do all things through Christ!

I am attracting the right people into my life!

I am an extraordinary creation!

I am a people builder!

I am always in the right place!

I am committed to being 100 percent debt-free!

I get things done!

I am destined to do great things!

I am worthy of my dreams!

I am worthy!

I am powerful!

God loves me!

I am fruitful!

I am fearfully and wonderfully made!

I am a winner!

I am prosperous!

I am generous!

I am humble!

I am joyful!

I am the apple of God's eye!

I am blessed and highly favored!

I have the desires of my heart!

I have all Your benefits!

I am forgiven!

I can rejoice every day!

My plans are successful!

I only speak life-giving words!

I am truthful!

I am powerful!

I am precious in Your sight!

I will not worry about anything!

I am exalted!

I am an overcomer!

I am a warrior!

I am set free!

I am filled with joy!

I am more than a conqueror!

I have a renewed mind!

I am patient and kind!

I am a beautiful and priceless treasure!

I am chosen by You!

I have a prosperous and hopeful future!

I can move mountains!

I am ready!

I am worth more!

I am God's child!

I am a friend of God!

I am a joint heir with Christ!

I am saved!

I have the mind of Christ!

I am a new creation!

I remove the words *I can't* from my vocabulary because *I can* do all things through Christ who gives me strength.

Chapter 4

Read, Declare, and Pray

The following pages contain twelve devotions that you can read, declare, and pray out loud over yourself and others. My prayer is that every scripture, declaration, and prayer will encourage you and uplift you. Read each one out loud. I've heard that when you hear what you are reading has more of an impact than just reading the words alone. May you experience the power of God's Word in your life as you read these devotions.

Devotion #1–Psalm 139:13–14

Read

Psalm 139:13–14: "For you created my inmost being, you knit me together in my mother's womb. I praise you because I am fearfully and wonderfully made."

Declare

I declare in Jesus' name that I am a masterpiece, I am loved, and I am a person of extreme value and significance!

I declare in Jesus' name that when God created me, He was well pleased with His creation and still is today!

I declare in Jesus' name that I am fearfully and wonderfully made. I am a child of God!

Pray

Lord, You knew me before You knit me together in my mother's womb. I thank You that just like when You created me, You are still well pleased with me, and You love me today. There is nothing anyone else can say to me to make me feel any different. I choose to believe what Your Word says about me. I give You all glory, honor, and praise that You are my God, and I am Your child. Thank You, Lord, for always being with me. I pray this in Jesus' mighty and powerful name. *Amen!*

Devotion #2–2 Timothy 1:7

Read

Second Timothy 1:7: "For God has not given us a spirit of fear, but of power and of love and of a sound mind."

Declare

I declare in Jesus' name that I have Jesus living in me, so fear cannot reside in me.

I declare in Jesus' name that I am strong and confident and able to do all things through Christ.

I declare in Jesus' name that greater is He that is in me than he that is in the world.

Pray

Lord, I may not always understand what is going on in my life or why, but I offer everything to You, knowing that You are always with me and that You will not give me more than I can handle. I put my trust in You, and I will not be afraid. I know that Your hand is always on me. I ask for Your wisdom and guidance in everything I do or face. Thank You, Lord, for always being with me. I pray this in Jesus' mighty and powerful name. *Amen!*

Devotion #3–Philippians 4:13

Read

Philippians 4:13: "I can do all things through Christ who strengthens me."

Declare

I declare in Jesus' name that I am more than a conqueror in Christ Jesus.

I declare in Jesus' name that nothing will keep me from the victory You have for me.

I declare in Jesus' name that I am a victor over my circumstances, not a victim of them.

Pray

Lord, I know that nothing is impossible with God. I thank You that You are my rock, my fortress, my strength, my shield, and my strong tower. I trust You, Lord, that no matter what challenge I face, I have already won. I have confidence because I know that You will never leave me or forsake me. I thank You that nothing the enemy puts before me will keep me from what You have for me. I give every second of my day to You and ask You to guide me through it. Thank You, Lord, for always being with me. I pray this in Jesus' mighty and powerful name. *Amen!*

Devotion #4–1 Peter 2:24

Read

First Peter 2:24: "He himself bore our sins in his body on the cross, so that we might die to sins and live for righteousness, 'by his wounds you have been healed.'"

Declare

I declare in Jesus' name that no matter what my mind may be telling me or my body may be feeling that God's Word is true, and I have been healed!

I declare in Jesus' name that every cell in my body must line up with the Word of God and that pain and sickness must leave my body now!

I declare in Jesus' name God's Word over my life, and I receive my healing!

Pray

Lord, I know this word is for me. I may be going through various physical or mental challenges right now, but I believe and declare what Your Word says that by Jesus' stripes, I have been healed. I declare in Jesus' name that my healing is complete. I thank You, Lord, for Your healing today. Thank You, Lord, for always being with me. I pray this in Jesus' mighty and powerful name. *Amen!*

Devotion #5–Proverbs 18:21

Read

Proverbs 18:21: "The tongue has the power of life and death, and those who love it will eat of its fruit."

Declare

I declare in Jesus' name that I will always be kind, respectful, and loving and will only speak words of life that will uplift and encourage!

I declare in Jesus' name that I will never speak words of death such as guilt, condemnation, belittlement!

I declare in Jesus' name that I will only speak words of life!

Pray

Lord, I pray that if at any time I am not speaking words of life to myself, my spouse, my children, my parents, my friends, my boss and coworkers, my doctors and medical staff, or anyone else, may God shut my mouth in Jesus' name like He shut the mouths of the lions when Daniel was in the lions' den. I choose from this moment forward to only speak words of life. I pray this in Jesus' mighty and powerful name. *Amen!*

Devotion #6–2 Corinthians 10:5

Read

Second Corinthians 10:5: "We demolish arguments and every pretension that sets itself up against the knowledge of God, and we take captive every thought to make it obedient to Christ."

Declare

I declare in Jesus' name that no evil thought can enter my mind!

I declare in Jesus' name that I will only speak godly thoughts that will bless, encourage, and lift up myself, my family, and everyone else I speak to!

I declare in Jesus' name that I will only speak life-giving words to everyone!

Pray

Lord, I give my mind to You today and ask You to renew it. I ask that You give me a heightened awareness of every thought that enters my mind, and I choose to take every thought captive to the obedience of Christ. I reject evil thoughts in the name of Jesus, and I only accept good thoughts. I choose to only speak good thoughts to myself, my family, and everyone else I speak to. Thank You, Lord, for always being with me. I pray this in Jesus' mighty and powerful name. *Amen!*

Devotion #7–Jeremiah 29:11

Read

Jeremiah 29:11: "'For I know the plans I have for you,' declares the Lord, 'plans to prosper you and not to harm you, plans to give you a hope and a future.'"

Declare

I declare in Jesus' name that no weapon formed against me will prosper, and everything that I touch prospers!

I declare in Jesus' name that my steps are ordered by the Lord, and He will always lead me down the right path!

I declare in Jesus' name that God has a plan for my life, and with Him, I will succeed!

Pray

Lord, my hope is in You. I believe that You have many good things in store for me and that You are leading me down the right path. I thank You that I am blessed, highly favored, victorious, strong, an extraordinary creation, and I am destined to do great things. I declare that I have a God-designed purpose and plan for my life, and I am who You say I am. With You, I cannot fail. Thank You, Lord, for always being with me. I pray this in Jesus' mighty and powerful name. *Amen!*

Devotion #8–Philippians 4:19

Read

Philippians 4:19: "My God will supply all your needs according to His riches and glory in Christ Jesus."

Declare

I declare in Jesus' name that God is my provider, and I lack nothing!

I declare in Jesus' name that my help comes from the Lord, Maker of heaven and earth!

I declare in Jesus' name that I have everything I need because God is my supplier!

Pray

Lord, I thank You that with You, I have everything I need. Like David said,

> The Lord is my shepherd, I lack nothing. He makes me lie down in green pastures, He leads me beside quiet waters, He restores my soul. You prepare a table in the presence of my enemies. You anoint my head with oil, my cup overflows. Surely goodness and mercy will follow me all the days of my life and I will dwell in the house of the Lord forever.

Thank You, Lord, for always being with me and providing for my needs. I pray this in Jesus' mighty and powerful name. *Amen!*

Devotion #9–Philippians 4:6

Read

Philippians 4:6: "Don't worry about anything; instead, pray about everything. Tell God what you need and thank Him for all He has done."

Declare

I declare in Jesus' name that I will not worry because He is with me!

I declare in Jesus' name that my help comes from the Lord, Maker of heaven and earth!

I declare in Jesus' name that I am a warrior and not a worrier; nothing can defeat me!

Pray

Lord, I thank You that I have not been given a spirit of fear, so I will not worry about any challenge or any circumstance that I may face. I know that I can come to You and ask for anything according to Your will, and it will be done. I am confident because my hope is in You. I thank You that You will never leave me nor forsake me. I thank You for all that You have done for me and will do for me in the future. I thank You that Your mercies are new every morning. I thank You that Your favor rests on me. Thank You, Lord, for always being with me. I pray this in Jesus' mighty and powerful name. *Amen!*

Devotion #10–Psalm 103:2–3

Read

Psalm 103:2–3: "Let all that I am praise the Lord. May I never forget the good things he does for me. He forgives all my sins and heals all my diseases."

Declare

I declare in Jesus' name that I will always worship the Lord. His praise shall continually be in my mouth!

I declare in Jesus' name that I will praise the Lord in all things, for He is worthy!

I declare in Jesus' name that I will praise the Lord continually for all He has done!

Pray

Lord, I thank You that I can come before You and praise You. Your Word says that You inhabit the praises of Your people, so I will praise You in all things. I praise You regardless of what is going on in my life because You give me joy, hope, and peace. I declare that nothing will ever steal my praise. I praise You for your love. I praise You for my loving family. I praise You for every blessing that You have ever given me or will give me in the future. I praise You because You are my rock and my fortress. I praise You for forgiving me and healing me. Thank You, Lord, for always being with me. I pray this in Jesus' mighty and powerful name. *Amen!*

Devotion #11–Isaiah 41:10

Read

Isaiah 41:10: "Don't be afraid for I am with you. Don't be discouraged for I am your God. I will strengthen you and help you. I will hold you up with my victorious right hand."

Declare

I declare in Jesus' name that nothing can defeat me because God is with me!

I declare in Jesus' name that, like David, I will slay every giant in my life because Your right hand is upon me!

I declare in Jesus' name that I am strong, courageous, and victorious through Christ!

Pray

Lord, I thank You that I don't have to be afraid or discouraged because You are always with me. I know that with You, I am victorious in everything that I face. I thank You that I am strong and courageous. I declare that I am more than a conqueror through Christ. My enemies cannot defeat me because You are with me, so I cry hallelujah to the Lamb of God. Blessed be the name of the Lord. You are always for me, so who can dare to be against me? No one. Thank You, Lord, for always being with me. I pray this in Jesus' mighty and powerful name. *Amen!*

Devotion #12–Proverbs 3:5–6

Read

Proverbs 3:5–6: "I trust in the Lord with all my heart, and I do not rely on my own understanding. I acknowledge the Lord in all my ways, and He promises to direct and make my paths straight."

Declare

I declare in Jesus' name that I will trust the Lord for wisdom and guidance in all things!

I declare in Jesus' name that I will take everything to God in prayer so I will make the right decisions!

I declare in Jesus' name that I will trust in the Lord always to guide and direct me!

Pray

Lord, I thank that You are with me in everything. Even though I may not understand everything that happens, I put my trust in You. I know that my steps are ordered by the Lord so I can stay on the right path. I ask You for wisdom and guidance. I know that Your thoughts are higher than my thoughts and Your ways are higher than my ways, so I will trust You to guide me. Thank You, Lord, for always being with me. I pray this in Jesus' mighty and powerful name. *Amen!*

Chapter 5

Turn Your Complaints into Praise

Has any of you ever been guilty of complaining about anything and everything that is wrong in the world and in your life? I know I have been. Has any of that complaining ever brought a smile to your face? I seriously doubt it.

What does complaining do? It invites stress, higher blood pressure, illness, disease, and so much more into your life and can make your life miserable and even shorten it. Who wants that? I know I don't.

Instead of complaining about anything and everything, how about turning those complaints into praise? Not only can it lower your stress and improve your health, and lengthen your life, and it can put a smile on your face. Say this out loud: I thank You, God, that I can always praise You!

Say Psalm 34:1–8 out loud:

> I will always bless the Lord; His praise shall continually be in my mouth. My soul shall make its boast in the Lord; Oh, magnify the Lord with me, and let us exalt His name together. I sought the Lord, and He heard me, and delivered me from all my fears. They looked to Him and were radiant, and their faces were not ashamed. This poor man cried out, and the Lord heard him, the angel of the Lord encamps all around those who fear Him and delivers them. Oh, taste and see that the Lord is good; blessed is the man who trusts in Him!

Prayer of Thanksgiving

Lift your hands to heaven and pray this prayer of thanksgiving out loud:

Lord, instead of complaining today, I choose to praise You and thank You.

I thank You, Lord, for Your love, Your mercy, and Your grace.

I thank You for Your goodness.

I thank You that even when others desert me, You are always with me.

I thank You that though others may be against me, You are always for me.

I thank You that even when I don't think I can accomplish anything good, You remind me that I can do all things through Christ who strengthens me.

I thank You that when my enemies try to bring harm to me or destroy me, You remind me that no weapon formed against me will ever prosper.

I thank You that when I am suffering any kind of lack in my life, You remind me that You will supply all my needs according to Your riches and glory in Christ Jesus.

I thank You that You are my rock and my refuge.

I thank You, Lord, that even though sickness and disease may try to attack me, I declare that by Jesus' stripes, I have been healed.

I thank You that Your goodness and mercy will follow me all the days of my life, and I will dwell in the house of the Lord forever.

Lord, I declare that from now on, no matter what is happening in my life or around me, I will not complain; instead, I will thank You and praise You that You are with me.

In Jesus' name, I pray, *amen*!

Chapter 6

Tithing–A Different Perspective

I want to talk about tithing. Now before your roll your eyes, or tune me out, or start doing things on your phone, please read what I have to say. We've all heard Malachi 3 verse 10 that says to bring your tithes into the storehouse, which is the church, which we should always do. You see, we've all been in places where tithing was either over preached or preached wrong to the point where we felt obligated to give instead of feeling compelled to give based on what God's Word says. The Bible says that God loves a cheerful giver.

Today, I would like you to see tithing from a different perspective. I think tithing goes beyond just giving money. Just like homes in a neighborhood have different shapes, the storehouse can take on different shapes as well, and the tithe can take on different forms. A tithe can be a word, deed, or action. Imagine this, what if the storehouse that you were supposed to tithe into at any given moment was another person's heart?

We have all done it, and I'm as guilty as anyone. We're walking through a store or somewhere, and instead of looking at a person approaching us, we look down or look for an item and ignore them like they're not even there. We don't know what that person is going through at that very moment; perhaps they're having a bad day or are in a bad relationship, lost their job or even their home, or got a bad report from the doctor. If we say something as simple as "Hi" or "How are you?" we just tithed into the storehouse of their heart without them even realizing it at that moment. Their response might be to ignore us, bite our head off for even asking, thank us, or start telling us what's going on in their life. Even if they ignore us or bite our heads off, at some point in the day, they may realize that you were the only person who was kind to them that entire day, and maybe they should have reacted differently. Even though it was just a little nugget, you tithed into the storehouse of their heart. Perhaps it's the person sitting next to you in church, a coworker, or your family. You can still tithe into their heart. Something as simple as a kind word, a smile, or perhaps touching their shoulder is all that person needed.

Proverbs 25:11 puts it this way, "Like apples of gold in settings of silver is a word aptly spoken." The people around us are settings of silver, and our words, deeds, or actions are the apples of gold. We have the power to give the people around us that aptly spoken word.

Proverbs 18:21 says, "The power of life and death is in the tongue and those that love it will eat its fruit." We can either tithe into the storehouse of someone's heart by speaking life, giving words, or we can rob the storehouse of a person's heart like Malachi 3 verse 8 says, "Would a man rob God?" We can rob the storehouse of a person's heart by speaking words of death. We can see that a person's storehouse is empty and contribute nothing to it. Something as simple as "Hi, how are you?" or "I love you" can put a little nugget into that storehouse.

First Samuel 15 verse 22 says, "To obey is better than sacrifice." By obeying God's Word and tithing into the storehouse of a person's heart, it could be the one thing that makes the difference between triumph or tragedy in a person's life.

When we are in church, we are like the apples of gold, and the people in the sanctuary are like the settings of silver. When we sing, whether we are in the choir or are in the congregation, we are not putting on a show, but what we are doing is we are tithing into the storehouse of the hearts, minds, and spirits of the people through our worship. Just the simple act of our worship could prepare someone to receive God's Word from the pastor, where otherwise, they may get nothing out of being in church no matter how good the message or anything else is. Our worship is that important. Let's tithe into the storehouses of people's hearts through our worship.

I'll conclude with this: whenever you are around anyone, whether it's your family, friends, coworkers, or complete strangers, be that apple of gold in settings of silver and tithe into the storehouse of their heart through your words, deeds, or actions.

Amen!

Chapter 7

A Prayer for Prosperity

Many of us have struggled with our finances at one time or another. We may have lost a job, or bought things we didn't need, or even paid too much for things. This is another area where we tend to beat ourselves up because it seems like we'll never climb out of the hole we dug for ourselves. When that happens, it's important to go to God's Word and read what it says about money and how to handle it. If we follow what the Bible says, we can climb out of that hole and never allow ourselves to fall into it again. If you're someone who has been in that situation, I invite you to pray the prayer below.

Father, in the name of Jesus, I lay my hands on the papers that list my debts and according to Romans 13:8, which says, "Let no debt remain outstanding, except for the continuing debt to love one another, for he who loves his fellowman has fulfilled the law." I repent forever being a bad representative financially of the gospel of Jesus Christ. I ask You to forgive me for any debts I created due to foolish decisions as well as the ones I did not. I choose to believe by faith that You will get me out of this debt and help me be a good steward of the money You provide from now on. You provide the grace, and I'll provide the man, and I'll pay every one of them if You get me the money. I choose to be a single-minded man according to James 1:5–6, where it says, "If any of you lacks wisdom, he should ask God, who gives generously to all without finding fault, and it will be given unto him. But when he asks, he must believe and not doubt, because he who doubts is like a wave in the sea, blown and tossed by the wind." I am your man, and I know that my riches come from you.

According to Matthew 18:19, where Jesus says, "Again, I tell you that if two of you on earth agree about anything you ask for, it will be done for you by my father in heaven," we are agreeing that I will have more than enough each month for me to operate my household. We declare according to Mark 11:23 and 24 that says,

> I tell you the truth, if anyone says to this mountain, "Go, throw yourself into the sea," and does not doubt in his heart but believes that what he says will happen, it will be done for him. Therefore, I tell you, whatever you ask for in prayer, believe that you have received it and it will be yours.

Thus, this mountain of debt must be gone and never return. I believe my daily bread is provided because God's Word says in 2 Corinthians 9:8, "And God is able to bless you abundantly, so that in all things at all times, having all that you need, you will abound in every good work." I believe it in my heart that I now receive it, we agree on it, and in the name of Jesus Christ of Nazareth from this day forward, I roll the cares of my income over on God, and this is my daily bread, and I thank You for it.

Father, I'm asking You in the name of Jesus to provide more than enough so that I can tithe, so that according to Malachi 3:10, which says, "Bring all the tithes (the whole tenth of your income) into the storehouse, that there may be food in My house, and prove

Me now by it, says the Lord of hosts, if I will not open the windows of heaven for you and pour out a blessing, that there shall not be room enough to receive it." Father, you said in Your Word according to Malachi 3:11, "I will rebuke the devourer [insects and plagues] for your sakes and he shall not destroy the fruits of your ground, neither shall your vine drop its fruit before the time in the field, says the Lord of hosts." Satan, I'm telling you in the name of my Lord Jesus, who is my bread provider, you get your affairs out of my home from this day forward. I declare in the name of Jesus that my house is a house of prosperity spiritually, mentally, physically, financially, and socially, and bless God, you get your dirty hands off my business and get off this premises, you don't have any right here, and the thieves and the stealers are not coming on this property anymore.

Father, I lose the powers of God on my life and my family's life according to Hebrews 1:13–14, which says, "Besides, to which angels has He ever said, Sit at My right hand [associated with Me in My royal dignity] till I make you enemies a stool for your feet? Are not all the angels ministering spirits (servants) sent out in the service [of God for the assistance] of those who are to inherit salvation?" Ministering spirits, in the name of Jesus, You go forth and cause my money to come, You garrison about my home, You protect my place, and You go before me every footstep that I take, every footstep that my children take, You protect and watch over them in the name of my Lord and Savior Jesus of Nazareth. Go cause my money to come in here like it is supposed to do.

Father, I praise You for your word in 3 John 2, which says, "Beloved, I pray that you may prosper in every way and [that your body] may keep well, even as [I know] your soul keeps well and prospers." So Father, in the name of Jesus of Nazareth, I praise You that I have received everything that I need in such abundance that my family and I will never lack for anything, and we will be able to serve You and others in a mighty way, and I praise You that because of Your generous abundance, I declare because of Your generous provision that I will be completely out of debt. I ask for Your wisdom and guidance to keep me from ever being in that place again.

Father, help me to always operate in forgiveness according to Mark 11:25–26. Help me to always operate in love according to 1 Corinthians 13.

In Jesus' name, I pray. Amen!

Afterword

Paul said in 2 Timothy 3:1–5,

> But mark this: There will be terrible times in the last days. People will be lovers of themselves, lovers of money, boastful, proud, abusive, disobedient to their parents, ungrateful, unholy, without love, unforgiving, slanderous, without self-control, brutal, not lovers of the good, treacherous, rash, conceited, lovers of pleasure rather than lovers of God, having a form of godliness but denying it's power. Have nothing to do with such people.

We have certainly seen a lot of this happening, and it seems to be on the increase. There seems to be a lot more negativity in the world today. My hope is that I can help change the way that people think about themselves and others. That was a big reason that I wrote *Yes You Are! Thoughts and Scriptures to Speak Over Yourself and Others*. I hope it blessed you as you read it as much as it blessed me to write it.

Thank you for taking the time to read *Yes You Are! Thoughts and Scriptures to Speak Over Yourself and Others*. I pray that you were uplifted and encouraged by this book. No matter what life may be throwing at you or what people may be telling you, always remember when it comes to what it says in God's Word about you: *Yes you are!*

Your comments regarding this book and how it impacted you are greatly appreciated.

You may send your comments to yesyouare2021@gmail.com.

I will be writing more *Yes You Are* books just like this one. If you have a favorite Bible scripture that uplifts and encourages you, please feel free to email me at yesyouare2021@gmail.com. It could get included in an upcoming *Yes You Are* book. I look forward to getting your feedback regarding this book. Please understand that due to the potential volume of emails that I may receive including duplicate scriptures, I may not be able to personally respond to each email; however, I am very grateful for each one that I do receive from you and will prayerfully consider each one to be put in an upcoming book.

May God bless you richly and give you His peace!

Team H.O.P.E.:
our mission is to Help Other People Everyday live
healthier and wealthier lives.

What are your goals in life? Do you want to have better health or better wealth, or both?
Keys to achieving goals:

- Create a goal and write it down.
- Set a deadline to accomplish it by.

Always remember:

- It is better to be on time than to be late.
- It is even better to be early than on time.

Watch this amazing one-minute video about a fourteen-year-old dog named Maggie.
What a difference the products made in this dog!
https://vimeopro.com/user32925383/maggie.
Imagine what they can do for you!

Three ways that you can learn more about how you can change your health and your wealth:
Go to https://americandream4me.com/successwarriors.

Send an email to successwarriors2021@gmail.com to join one of our weekly calls.

Write to:

Team H.O.P.E.

P.O. Box 970

Thermopolis, WY 82443

Connect with me online:

Facebook: https://www.facebook.com/bigdreams4u

My Facebook group: Yes You Are!

My business page: https://www.facebook.com/adnwyoming

LinkedIn: https://linkedin.com/in/bigdreams4u

Twitter: https://twitter.com/bigdreams4u2021

CPSIA information can be obtained
at www.ICGtesting.com
Printed in the USA
LVHW020619270722
724372LV00013B/369

9 781685 567934